D0341052

FIVE SECONDS AT A TIME

FIVE SECONDS AT A TIME

HOW LEADERS MAKE THE IMPOSSIBLE POSSIBLE

DENIS SHACKEL, PhD
with TARA BRADACS

Collins

Published by Collins, an imprint of HarperCollins Publishers Ltd.

First edition

HarperCollins books may be purchased for educational, business, or sales promotional use through our Special Markets Department.

HarperCollins Publishers Ltd
2 Bloor Street East, 20th Floor
Toronto, Ontario, Canada
M4W 1A8

www.harpercollins.ca

Library and Archives Canada Cataloguing in Publication

Shackel, Denis
Five seconds at a time : how leaders can make the impossible possible / Denis Shackel with Tara Bradacs.

ISBN 978-1-55468-794-7

1. Leadership. 2. Success in business. 3. Shackel, Denis.
4. Mountaineering accidents—New Zealand—Ruapehu, Mount.
I. Bradacs, Tara II. Title.
HD38.2.S53 2010   658.4'09   C2010-900513-9

Printed and bound in Canada

DWF 9 8 7 6 5 4 3 2 1

For my beloved sister, Kathleen,
and her husband, Bruce MacGregor

The last photograph of Bruce

"*There amid the anxiety, fear, blood, sadness, exhaustion, torment, isolation, and fatigue, is an outstretched hand—another existence, proffering a 'transfusion of energy, encouragement, and instructional wisdom from a seemingly external source.' A presence appears, a Third Man who, in the words of legendary Italian climber Reinhold Messner, 'leads you out of the impossible.'*"

—John Geiger, *The Third Man Factor*

CONTENTS

FOREWORD

For each of us, there comes at least one moment when we find ourselves at a personal or professional crossroad. We make a decision that defines our future, whether or not we are aware of it at the time. In that moment, all the work we have done to develop and nourish our character, values and principles, knowledge and skills is realized. For Denis Shackel, that moment came when he made the decision to continue his climb up, rather than down, the mountain.

I have known Denis, who leads our Communications Faculty team at Ivey, for the past five years as both a colleague and a friend. Many of us at the School have had the privilege of hearing first-hand the story of his experience on Mount Ruapehu in New Zealand. It is now an anchor to an excellent three-day program, open to the public, called *Leadership, Persuasion and Influence through Communications*.

Although I have heard his inspiring story of loss, love and courage on more than one occasion, it never fails to linger for days as I ponder the question "What would I have done?"

For the past six years, my focus has been the development of one form of leadership—*business* leadership. These years have marked a time of soul-searching for me and for many others, both in the business world and in business schools. After a series of crises over the decade, culminating in the near collapse of our financial system in the fall of 2008, business leadership has come under intense scrutiny. It has become clear that significant changes have taken place in the demands placed on business leaders as they respond to a rapidly changing global environment. Leadership itself is changing.

With globalization, a growing integration of markets, and the rapid advance of technology and information systems, business is brimming with opportunities and endless possibilities but also with new and very complex challenges. Today, effective leaders need the ability to anticipate and quickly adapt to change. Perhaps most important, in this new, flattened world, standout leaders are no longer found in the corner office alone. Leadership happens throughout the enterprise, from top to bottom; we are all leaders, no matter what our title.

Today's leaders must be exceptional team players. More than ever, they must be able to influence and persuade those over whom they have no power. They need to build, foster and influence a complex web of relationships across all levels—from employees, partners and suppliers to customers, citizens and even competitors. Leaders need a solid understanding of business units across the enterprise—an enterprise that may include offices in a number of diverse cultures and political realities. Today's great leaders engender trust, encourage initiative and secure loyalty. We call this new form of leadership Cross-Enterprise Leadership™.

Does that seem a tall order for any one person? It shouldn't. Leadership does not begin when you scan your badge at the office door. Leadership begins when you wake up, look in the bathroom mirror, and decide on your attitude towards the morning, and it continues with each role you take on throughout the day. Leadership is really about choosing how to manage your life. It is a personal choice.

Denis's book has arrived just in time to return us to the fundamentals of personal leadership—the principles, practices and habits that define a life well lived and result in career goals that become career achievements and dreams that take flight. I was particularly taken with Denis's central message—to slow down, even for just five seconds. Stepping back is an integral part of the process of moving forward, particularly in crisis situations.

Martin Luther King Jr. once said, "The ultimate measure of a man is not where he stands in moments of comfort and convenience, but where he stands in times of challenge and controversy." As an educator, I have often been asked what I do when I find myself in crisis, or when black and white dissolve into a murky grey. There is no easy answer. The best thing you can do, I tell my students, is to slow things down. Step off the treadmill. Look with the eyes of an outsider at what is going on in the organization. Consult with people you trust. Most important, listen to your heart. If it doesn't *feel* right, it probably isn't—no matter what anybody is telling you. This clarity does not happen by accident. It comes from a foundation of knowing who you are. Your compass must recognize true north in order to find it. So whether intuition or spiritual inspiration is your guiding light in a moment of crisis, it evolves from a strong foundation of principles, values and beliefs developed long before that moment.

When Denis asked me what I thought of the idea of developing *Five Seconds at a Time,* the story of his Mount Ruapehu experience, into a practical and accessible book on leadership, I gave a resounding "Yes!" Denis is an award-winning faculty member at the Ivey Business School who transforms the classroom into a living laboratory in which students are challenged to know themselves first, so that they may communicate their message most effectively to others. Experience, we believe, is the best way to develop the wisdom and sound judgment leaders need in the real world. If anyone could transform that experience into a book, I knew it would be Denis.

Five Seconds at a Time is meant to be experienced, not simply read. It is a book designed to transform your corporate meeting room, favourite café or family living room into a classroom. It is a book meant to be shared with colleagues, friends and family. Read the book, and when your moment comes, you'll be ready.

Dean Carol Stephenson, O.C.
Lawrence G. Tapp Chair in Leadership
Richard Ivey School of Business
University of Western Ontario

1

THE CLIMB

"Hey, Bruce, your crampon's falling off!"

As my beloved brother-in-law turned to look at his boot, I didn't imagine for a second that he would instantly lose his balance and begin a 3,000-foot, 100-mile-an-hour plummet to his death at the foot of the glacier.

Bruce and I had planned this mountain climb several years before. At the time, we had talked excitedly of conquering the tallest peak in New Zealand, Mount Cook (12,316 feet), and of hoping to join those who had overcome the considerable difficulties involved. But many had died in attempting this climb. As husbands and fathers, we decided that pursuing this particular dream might be irresponsible, so we would instead share a less dangerous adventure. Mount Ruapehu, at 9,177 feet, is recognized as not too onerous a climb, and furthermore, Bruce, who had already climbed it several times, fondly referred to it as his favourite mountain. This was the backdrop to the moment in which I found myself gazing down the glacier upon which Bruce had spent his last few earthly moments.

As the horror of the moment exploded in my mind, the reality in which I found myself struck me like a sledgehammer. First to register in my racing brain was a surprisingly clear picture of a small white spot moving along the winding road that led away from the foot of the mountain. This tiny object was the van driven by my sister, Kathleen. The three of us had camped the previous night at the end of the road so that Bruce and I could start our memorable expedition before sunrise. The plan was for Kathleen to drive the camper around the base of the mountain and pick us up at the agreed-upon spot between five and six that evening. Until now, everything had gone as planned. We had excitedly awoken early, double-checked our gear, enjoyed a satisfying breakfast and begun our ascent, all before daybreak.

Bruce was not only an exceptional husband to Kathleen but also an unusually compassionate, empathetic and selfless man. He had insisted on carrying the pack containing our water, food and medical supplies during our ascent, as well as the layers of clothing we shed as the temperatures rose. In his typically meticulous way, he also had me demonstrate to him, once we reached the snow line, that I remembered from my earlier climbing experiences how to break a fall using my ice axe.

Immediately prior to my startled observation that the spikes on his right boot appeared broken, Bruce had been cheering me on in his typically positive manner. I had climbed to about 8,000 feet under his guidance, encouragement and instruction. Now I had to surmount a particularly steep and, for me, challenging few feet of the glacier to a rock that was protruding through the surface of the snow and on which Bruce was standing, looking down at me. He was still about twenty feet higher than I was when I made it to the lower end of the rock. I banged its icy cover with my axe as Bruce had taught me. Stepping onto the stability of the ice-free surface, I yelled up an exuberant "We did it! Thanks, brother!"

It was at this point that I realized that Bruce did not have stable footing under his right boot and my nightmare officially began. I will never forget the moments immediately following Bruce's stumble. There was a muffled *bang* as the pack strapped to his back hit the surface of the glacier. He then began a feet-first descent toward me with unbelievable speed. He was slightly to my left, and as he came rocketing down, I instinctively thrust out my left hand to catch him. Seeing my extended hand, Bruce stuck out his. Of the more than two billion seconds I have been alive, there is one second I will never forget. As the gap between our hands shrank with lightning speed, our eyes connected for a split second, and we realized what appeared imminent. Bruce pulled his hand back and, in so doing, allowed me to write this story. While we hadn't had time to exchange words, I am absolutely sure we both recognized that had he accepted my outstretched hand, his momentum would have yanked me off the rock and he'd have taken me with him. Bruce's extraordinary love was the main reason I described him at his funeral as "the most Christ-like man I've ever met." These last few seconds of my seeing Bruce alive are engraved in my memory. I will never forget them for the rest of my days.

After Bruce disappeared from my sight beyond a rock immediately below me, I fleetingly lost consciousness out of shock. Once I came to, fortunately still clutching the rock, I assumed that the task ahead of me was to climb downward to the level where Bruce had stopped his fall, to help him regain his stability so we could continue on our shared journey. Little did I realize that he was now with his Creator and my task was more realistically that of survival. It was about eleven o'clock when I began my descent, studying any area where Bruce could possibly be.

By about one o'clock, I felt anxious. By two, I began to panic. By three, I was desperate. By four, I simply couldn't comprehend how I had not yet found Bruce. All that my bewildered mind could fathom was that the clear and uninterrupted view of the mountain face below me did not include evidence of Bruce's presence or even of his slide. (It wasn't until the close of the following day that I learned that the rare conditions of that particular week in mid-May had turned the ice and snow into a steel-like surface impenetrable to the spike of Bruce's ice axe. I will always graphically see and hear his axe spike screeching along the surface of the mountain.)

Emotionally and physically exhausted, I rested for a few minutes on a "de-iced" rock. Having spent more than four hours looking for Bruce, I felt grief in my failure to find him. And now the incoming clouds were beginning to obscure the valley below, preventing a clear view of anything farther than about fifty feet. *What do I do now?* I thought. *Should I continue going farther down looking for him or assume I must have somehow missed him and begin climbing back up?*

At this point of fatigue and disillusion, I believe it was intuition that prompted me to scramble back up the mountain. I have no concrete proof or rational explanation for this conviction but now understand why writer Warren Bennis has referred to intuition as a "blessed impulse." The urge to climb upward was dominant. Minutes before he slipped, Bruce had mentioned the existence of a hut anchored into the face of the glacier very near the mountain's summit. The thought that the hut might house a means of sounding an alarm seemed secondary to the strong pull to head upward.

Whether it was right or wrong, the decision to climb up proved to be one that, I believe, shaped the remainder of my life. It has been said that in our moments of decision, our destiny is determined. My choice launched me into another chapter of this memorable day. I don't recall how long it took or, for that matter, how I regained the height from which Bruce had slipped, but I somehow managed to do so as the sun began to hide behind the side of the mountain. Then began another series of experiences that have also contributed to changing my life.

I could see the hut. To my despair, not only was it considerably higher and to the left of where I'd calculated it to be; it also perched beyond a wall of ice. At this point, I heard words that I unequivocally believe were spoken to me by God himself—words I had heard before but whose exact source I could not place. Yes, I knew they were from Scripture, and I may even have guessed they were spoken by Saint Paul, but I wasn't certain. From behind me and above my right shoulder clearly came the words "I can do all things through Christ who strengthens me." Some might argue that my brain had simply kicked in with information that had been stored there since my Sunday-school days. Or that the words came to me as a consequence of my efforts over recent years to memorize certain Biblical quotes. But I prefer the reasoning that God offered me profound words of encouragement and a gracious reminder of where my real strength lay. Even today, I have no earthly explanation of how I managed to climb the ten-foot ice wall and eventually grab hold of the wooden supports anchoring the hut into the face of the mountain.

Around six o'clock, I reached the hut. After momentarily collapsing against one of its buttresses and then crawling around to its front, I discovered the hut was used infrequently to say the least. A good eight inches of ice blocked the doorway—my first clue that although I had attained this goal, the search for a means to call for help, which had played a role in motivating my climb back up the glacier, was unlikely to be successful.

Once I was inside, my spirits fell even lower. There was definitely no phone. In fact, the large storage cupboards, all conveniently labelled—Blankets, Ropes, Supplies—were empty! I opened storage box after storage box and found nothing but dirty floorboards staring up at me. And then I glimpsed a locked cupboard. A few swings of the ice axe broke the hinges. I pulled out an oblong metal tin with the label Four Rations Food taped on the outside.

The spikes on my boots made quick work of prying open the soldered lid to reveal four tins of spaghetti, five candles, a box of matches and a tube of honey marked New Zealand Army. While I did later squeeze some honey into my mouth, it was not what I craved. I would have given almost anything for the water bottles in Bruce's pack. I felt dizzy and overwhelmingly exhausted, and I believe my raging thirst contributed to these feelings. Then I spotted a single can of beer—New Zealand Steinlager, my favourite brand—perched on one of the two-by-four supports between the wall studs. A sudden gift brought by an angel of mercy! My inclination was to not only grab it but gulp it down. With supernatural restraint, I punctured the can with my crampon and poured the drink through the cracks of the floorboards. I knew the alcohol would make me dehydrated, so the beer was potentially more harmful than useful. The empty can, however, was very useful and became instrumental in my eventual rescue.

I also found a fibreglass toboggan—the sort used to carry (slide) an injured person down a slope. Attached to the shell was a bright orange liner that would be used to wrap the patient in and some rope, meant to secure his or her body. The toboggan itself wasn't of use to me, but I thought the liner could prove valuable because of its colour. I secured the rope to the door frame of the hut and, with a gentle push, slid the toboggan down the mountain. The rope was about twenty feet long, and I thought the orange splash against the snow might draw attention to my whereabouts. (I never learned whether or not it was spotted.)

It was now almost dark, and with the temperature rapidly plummeting, I mourned not only the water bottles in Bruce's pack but also the warm clothing. The supply of spaghetti (also opened with my boot spikes) proved worthless, as rust had formed on the inside of each tin. But at least with the contents thrown out, a container could hold the five candles. Thankfully, the matches still worked, and I was able to dispel the ominous darkness. In another spaghetti tin, I melted the ice chipped from the doorway and created drinking water. While I had finally quenched my thirst, my even greater need was somehow to deal with the already freezing temperature, which was gradually dropping even further. Dressed in shorts, a T-shirt and a sunhat, I could think of only one thing to do: jump up and down beneath the peak of the hut to keep my blood flowing. My mind did not give up on jumping, but my body eventually did. I collapsed on the floor.

I'm not sure how long I lay on the floorboards, my teeth chattering uncontrollably, before something prompted me to pull myself up onto one of the cupboards. From there, the flickering light of a single candle drew my attention to a makeshift table against the wall. On this rough square of plywood supported by a couple of two-by-four legs lay a book, which I recognized when I looked more closely as the Holy Bible, incredibly put there through the work of the Gideon Bible Society.

In awe of the tenacity and commitment of the Gideons, I picked up the book. The candle offered enough light for me to read by. A single typed page, glued inside the front cover of this blue, cloth-bound volume, listed various human emotional conditions and suggested specific passages relevant to each state. I recall reading, "In times of joy, turn to page . . . ," "In times of sadness, turn to page . . . ," along with similar entries for loss, worry, fear and so on. The line that called out to me at that moment read, "In times of despair, turn to page 1,048." I followed the instructions and will never forget the goosebump response that was clearly not related to my shivering. There, on the right-hand page, at the top of the right-hand column, a verse leaped off the page as if emblazoned: "I can do all things through Christ who strengthens me." I now know that the actual reference is Philippians 4:13, but outside on the glacier, only about three hours earlier, when I had heard those same words, I could not have named the source.

The result was absolute confidence that I was not alone up there and the assurance that if I were to freeze to death before morning, I was ultimately being looked after and watched over by God himself. Although this knowledge did not even begin to ease my physical discomfort in the bone-rattling temperature of thirty degrees below, my spirits were lifted and my hope rekindled. I certainly credit my attitude, my positive thinking and my faith for my survival.

A number of other "coincidences," which I believe were supernaturally engineered, saved my life. The wonder of reading the very words I'd heard earlier inspired my hope and increased my adrenaline sufficiently for me to persevere through the cold. The air by this point was so desperately frigid that on each inhalation, I felt as if pins and needles were spiking into my lungs. I held each breath for as long as I could in an attempt to warm it up even a little bit, and then I would reluctantly expel it to the count of five. After thanking God for those five seconds, I repeated the behaviour. The principle underlying this repetition was that of breaking the time down into small, manageable pieces. I got through the longest night of my entire life *five seconds at a time.*

The first rays of dawn seemed to pop suddenly into my consciousness. They also seemed to disappear just as quickly at least two or three times before my confused mind could believe that they really were sunrays and proof that I had made it through the night.

Now began a period that, strangely, felt even longer than the hours spent in pitch darkness. (I had blown out the candles in order to preserve them in case I'd needed to melt more ice.) After what had seemed an eternity of waiting and fighting the feeling that I was drowning—a fear I'd had since childhood—I opened the door to allow the light now creeping over the horizon to enter the hut. I kept assuring myself that my sister, Kathleen, would have sounded the alarm, and rescue people would be out looking for me. Sure enough, not long afterward, as I lay on the floor shivering uncontrollably, I heard the undeniable sound of helicopter blades. It was approximately seven o'clock.

Stumbling out, I clutched the door frame and felt a rush of relief when the throbbing crystallized into the image of a helicopter appearing from the far side of the peak. The night before, I'd created a signalling device using the inner shiny surface of the Steinlager can, pried apart with the crampons from one of my boots. It seemed as though it would be an adequate mirror to draw attention to my location. With what I thought was reasonable accuracy, I attempted to signal the pilot. But at the point when the chopper moved close enough for me to decipher the large letters R–E–S–C–U–E painted on the fuselage, the unbelievable happened. The helicopter turned sharply and disappeared in the direction from which it had come! I "lost it" at this point, crying out in disbelief and sobbing inconsolably as I crumpled onto the hard floor. So near, yet so far . . .

I may have lost consciousness, but it couldn't have been for long. The next thing I knew, I heard the pounding sound of the chopper again, although it died down abruptly, its pitch lowered enough to suggest to my stunned mind that it may have landed somewhere close by. Another surge of hope and rush of adrenaline enabled me to stagger yet again to the door, thinking that perhaps I *had* been seen. I recall praying that the rescue team would bring ropes, because I knew I would be unable to walk any distance without assistance. When the helicopter reappeared heading in my direction, I abandoned my mirror and waved my arms with every ounce of energy left in me. The machine hovered only about two feet above the glacier. Although I didn't see the door open on the far side, I caught sight of two pairs of legs dangling from the chopper. They materialized into two full bodies that touched down onto the ice surface and moved around the tail of the helicopter toward me. To say I gave these angels of mercy a warm reception is perhaps the understatement of my life! Grateful to my core, I collapsed into their arms. They poured hot chocolate into me and asked whether I was Bruce or Denis. A sickening, hot rush of relief swept over me as the chopper whisked me back to a base camp, where a medical crew gave me more hot chocolate and skilful, gentle care as I was plied with questions so they could determine where to start looking for Bruce.

It turned out that the rescue party was initially composed of as many people as the helicopter could fit (the more pairs of eyes, the better), leaving no room for me once I'd been spotted, which explained why the chopper had left and come back again. Later that day, after I'd been rushed to the hospital for a checkup—where I learned that not only would I not lose any fingers or toes but, miraculously, I hadn't even suffered any frostbite—I did tactfully suggest to my rescuers that a small wave of recognition would have prevented my being subjected to a last-minute cliff-hanger of despair. However, they did save my life, and I can now smile at the relatively insignificant oversight.

I will never forget watching through the window of the base camp as the helicopter returned about twenty minutes after the medical team had gotten me bundled up. Even before the blades had stopped spinning, the pilot jumped out. He ran to the building and, as he opened the door, announced the razor-sharp news: "Found him. He's dead." The blow of the words I didn't want to hear initially left me breathless and speechless. In hindsight, their delivery was further evidence of the crew's wisdom and skill. If you have to be cut, better to have it done with a sharp knife than a slow, blunt instrument. Bruce was found with only half of his skull intact, which means he died instantly upon impact and didn't suffer.

The events that followed—the heart-bursting reunion with Kathleen, the grief and agony of losing Bruce and the pervasive question of "Why, Lord?"—amplified the profound significance of my May 17, 1997, experience. My internal voice generates a conviction that I was picked up by the helicopter so that I could enter a new chapter in my life, a chapter that God had planned. It simply wasn't yet my time to join Bruce. There was still work for me to complete here on earth. And so, here, I write about it.

My epiphany was not on the road to Damascus but at the top of Mount Ruapehu, located near the centre of New Zealand's North Island. When one is facing death, life takes on a new perspective. In my case, ideas and principles that I had regarded for most of my life simply as common sense suddenly stood out with remarkable and renewed significance.

I have chosen to share the profoundly personal narrative of my mountaintop experience, but by no means am I trying to exploit my tragedy. The lessons I have learned from this event have taken shape over several years of reflection. I am sharing them because I believe they can have a positive influence in the lives of others.

In its own right, this is a story of courage and love, a testimony to the grace of God as well as to the heroism of my beloved coach and brother-in-law, Bruce. My experience could be read as a stand-alone account of adventure, survival and inspiration. However, it is my hope that you will also regard it as a case study of sorts that offers guidelines to *charismatic leadership, business success* and *fruitful living,* particularly in the face of seemingly impossible challenges.

This book will unveil the "secrets" that enabled me to survive the longest night of my life. It is my conviction that the principles, practices and habits that saved my life are the same principles, practices and habits that all leaders must implement to be successful in achieving their greatest hopes and dreams. We all live through times when we feel overwhelmed by our circumstances or suffer feelings of deep doubt, perhaps even despair. My goal is for my story to enable you to step back so you can see clearly before you step forward to turn the seemingly impossible into the possible.

My story and lessons learned are personal and disclose beliefs largely of a spiritual nature, which do not generally appear in texts on leadership, influence, power or business success. My intention is not to manipulate or convert readers to my particular belief system. However, I have become convinced that leadership is a journey toward integrity, a holistic union of body, mind and soul and, therefore, a spiritual journey. I believe that the power of great leadership is a phenomenon that others feel in a leader's presence because of who that person is, what he or she stands for and where he or she is going, rather than simply a set of learned or practised behaviours.

My desire is that this text will reflect my walking my own talk. Other writers support my belief that leadership starts on the *inside* and that it is only when we align our personal values with our actions that we generate the personal leadership power that makes it possible for us to help others do the same. I see my role as one of reminding rather than instructing; there is nothing distinctly new about these principles and practices. But they certainly enabled me to step from a seemingly impossible situation to one of not only survival but, ultimately, great benefit and success. When leaders internalize and implement these ideals, they too can learn to achieve the seemingly impossible.

2

FIVE SECONDS AT A TIME
REFLECTION

"A journey of a thousand miles begins with a single step."
—*Lao-tzu*

Have you ever felt ready to give up? That you simply can't go on? Have you ever felt so overwhelmed that you don't know where to begin—as if you are engulfed in a cloud of fog, unable to see the way? I know exactly what this lifelessness, exhaustion and anguish feels like. I have been blessed with the gift of life. It is now my mission to help you find your way up the mountain, not only for you to survive but also for you to accomplish what at first may seem impossible.

How did I stay alive, stranded on a glacier and dressed in only a T-shirt and shorts? As night fell on the mountain, the air became so cold that it felt as if hundreds of pins and needles were stabbing my lungs. To try to warm the air I inhaled, I held each breath for as long as I could. When forced to breathe out, I counted "one, two, three, four, five." I then gave thanks to God for getting me through those five seconds and repeated the practice. I didn't stay alive for the eight-hour night, but rather I stayed alive for five seconds—5,760 times.

I used the five-seconds counting pattern at numerous points during my mountaintop journey. It helped me to "step back" (pause) and break down the seemingly impossible journey into manageable intervals; it was, therefore, critical to my survival. As I climbed the mountain toward the hut, I deliberately took "perspective breaks," during which I divided the ultimate distance I had to cover into segments of approximately fifteen to twenty feet—wherever a protruding rock indicated a convenient "chapter." I then broke this chapter into sentences, the sentences into words, and then with exceptional focus and attention to minute detail, I broke each word into syllables. Ironically, it was Bruce who taught me how to break down the journey into pieces. During the initial part of our climb, he diligently taught me how to make shelves to rest on by banging the rock with my ice pick to make a de-iced surface.

Stepping Back by Using the Five Seconds at a Time Technique

So where do you start when you are ready to give up and feel as though you simply can't go on? Only when the route to a desired outcome is broken into manageable and realistic bites can the seemingly impossible be accomplished. The first step requires an internal "stepping back" in order to then step forward.

visualization + self talk
perspective breaks.

> ## THE FIVE SECONDS AT A TIME TECHNIQUE
>
> BREATHE AND PAUSE TO REFLECT on the goal, how
> you feel and whether you are still headed in the
> right direction. (This often happens between the
> steps below as well.)
>
> PRIORITIZE what's most important (the big rocks).
>
> BREAK DOWN top priorities into manageable
> intervals or tasks (big rocks into stones)
> with specific timelines assigned to each.
>
> ACKNOWLEDGE when tasks along the way
> (stepping stones) have been accomplished
> and reward yourself when they have.

To give an example of the Five Seconds at a Time concept, I have asked numerous clients and students over the past ten years to step back by asking them the question, "How do you eat an elephant?" (The answer will be revealed at the end of this chapter.)

Breathing and Pausing to Reflect on the Goal
Too often we try to pack so much into a day that we experience the disappearance of pauses. By losing moments during which we could catch our breath, we forgo the time to ponder our actions, goals and priorities. Have you ever felt glued to

your desk? Too busy to eat lunch? Author Paul Boers reflects, "Those of us concerned about living out our faith, fostering compassion and working for justice need to pay attention. To act according to our best instincts, we need sanctuaries of space and time to reflect on our deepest values and pay attention to the deepest thing we know. Our wide culture, too, needs opportunities for slowing down."[1]

Our overscheduled generation races through one task as quickly as possible so we can get to the next. We hurry up to relax and then can't seem to relax at all.

One Friday evening, for example, Rebecca, a good friend of mine, called me in tears. She'd stayed at work until six thirty to try to catch up on her to-do list after a hectic week. That day at work, she'd envisioned having a quiet, romantic, candlelit dinner at home with her husband. So Rebecca rushed through traffic to the grocery store and picked up items to make a nice home-cooked meal. By the time she got home and unpacked the groceries, it was seven forty-five (thirty minutes commuting, thirty minutes shopping and a quick stop to get a bottle of wine). The house was an absolute mess because of her hectic week, and she was starving. Rebecca's husband, John, also had to work late and had also just walked in the door. Rebecca explained to me that she had an emotional breakdown because she'd wanted to have a nice dinner ready and was now too exhausted to make it or even to enjoy the evening. She felt frustrated that she had used up all her energy on work and errands and had nothing left for her husband.

After some quiet reflection the next day, Rebecca shared with me her realization that it was unrealistic to think she could juggle all those tasks in one day. She'd put unnecessary pressure on herself. As a result, her biggest rock (her spouse) didn't get the focus it deserved. She should have either left work earlier or picked up some healthy takeout for the romantic dinner. Had Rebecca stepped back and taken five seconds to pause and re-evaluate before she left work that Friday night, the outcome would have been dramatically different.

Regularly, slow down and ask yourself, "Are my expectations realistic?" If you are open to exploring or developing your faith, ask, "What are God's expectations of me?" It puts me at ease knowing that God puts people first and offers "perfect peace" during stressful times. It is also refreshing to take a pause, be alone with your own breath and feel it go in and out, all while listening to your soul and reflecting on how you feel. I did this at several points during my search for Bruce. I discuss this concept further in Chapter 4.

These five-second intervals create not only pauses for re-evaluation but also opportunities to listen intuitively. In his book *Timelock,* Ralph Keyes suggests the following techniques for creating necessary downtime[2]:

- Treat delays as found time.
- Take an occasional soak in the bath.
- When hurried, ask yourself, "Do I really need to rush? What's the worst thing that can happen if I don't? Is that worse than what it's costing me to hurry?"
- Make a conscious effort to not always take the

faster path. For example, walk when possible, rather than drive.

- Reduce background noise, which often contributes to a hectic feeling and makes it hard to hear important information.
- Listen to your body—it's giving you good advice.

Attempting to schedule every minute of the day only increases tension while reducing effectiveness. Not only does pausing allow us time to slow down and reflect, it also increases our productivity. Have you ever been so focused on a task or project that your productivity was hindered? I recently read a dog-and-bone analogy that seems relevant here. A chain-link fence separates a dog from a juicy bone. "The dog desperately wants to get that bone, and so it paws and scratches frantically at the fence. But no matter how hard it tries, the dog just can't get through. . . . It drives the dog crazy because the bone is so close yet remains just out of reach. Yet, if the dog would only take its eyes off the bone for a moment and look to its left—six feet away—it would see an open gate."[3]

One of my MBA students recently wrote me an encouraging letter after completing one of my classes. She said, "Thank you for teaching me life skills to overcome challenges, to 'seize the day,' and to believe in myself and in my abilities. Thank you for making me more aware of how to treat others. Thank you for making me self-reflect and take a step back from life's everyday details and see the bigger picture."[4] Next time you are faced with something difficult, step back and pause before you act. Take at least five seconds to reflect on the issue from a broader view. Use this time to look at the whole forest and not just the trees. This will help you gain a clearer perspective before you step forward to face an overwhelming challenge.

Prioritizing the Big Rocks

So how do we break down life's challenges into smaller, more manageable tasks? How do we determine what the first step should be?

I recently used the following powerful illustration to teach business students the concept of prioritization. I placed a large glass jar on a table at the front of the classroom. I gave my fifteen students one fist-sized rock each and had them come up one by one to place the rocks in it. I knew that no more than twelve rocks would fit into it. When the thirteenth student came up to place his rock in the jar and discovered there was no room, I asked the class, "Is the jar full?" Predictably, most of the students called out or nodded "Yes." "Really?" I asked. Some students looked puzzled; others were deep in thought. As I paused to let the students reflect, I heard some speak out, "Yes, the jar is full."

I then reached under the desk and pulled out a bucket of gravel. I poured in the gravel and shook the jar so the pieces could settle into the spaces between the big rocks. I asked the class again, "Is the jar full?" Starting to catch on to my demonstration, the students hesitated. "Probably not," one student blurted out.

"Good!" I replied as I reached back under the desk and brought out a container of sand. I added the sand to the mix in the jar. It seeped into the spaces between the rocks and gravel. Once more I asked the question, "Is the jar full?" "No!" someone shouted out.

I grabbed a pitcher of water and filled the jar to the brim. Then I asked the class, "What is the point of this illustration?" One eager student raised her hand. "No matter how full your schedule is, if you try really hard, you can always fit more things in." "No," I replied, "that's not the main point."

The truth this illustration teaches us is that *if you don't put the big rocks in first, you will never get them in at all.*[5]

In breaking down our challenges and tasks into smaller, manageable bites, it is important to step back to figure out what the big bites are, so that we can put them in the jar, or tackle them, first. Thus, Five Seconds at a Time can be paralleled to five big rocks at a time. Five Seconds at a Time is about stepping back to the basics. Prioritizing your "big rocks" will help you do this. What are the big rocks in your life? Time with your loved ones? Your faith? Your education? What are the big rocks in your work? Or in a problem you are facing? If you don't put the big rocks in first, you won't get them in at all. If you worry about the small stuff (the gravel, the sand—i.e., the housework, the laundry, the filing, etc.), then you'll fill your life stressing over little things that don't really matter, leaving you without the time you need for the big, important stuff.

The reality is that resources are limited, so it's crucial to distinguish between the *need-to-have* and the *nice-to-have* goals. It will be helpful for you to identify criteria for the big rocks.

These criteria will help you differentiate high priority goals from low priority ones. For example, which goals or activities

- are time-sensitive (that is, have deadlines that cannot be extended)?
- will have the largest impact?
- are most aligned with your skill set?
- will your manager, organization or family value most?
- are proactive and will help you recognize opportunities or prevent "firefighting" in the future?
- will be overly time-consuming (that is, the time investment may outweigh the results)?
- are aligned with your own personal values?
- will be most personally fulfilling and most enjoyable?
- are fulfilling career goals at the expense of your family priorities?
- could be considered an early or easy win to build momentum for future tasks?

Take a moment (or more) to reflect on your big rocks and your sand or gravel.

A great way to determine the priority level of your big rocks is through a prioritization selection matrix. This tool allows you to select criteria that are important to you, assign an importance rating and then rank the criteria against each priority, or big rock. The output is a numeric calculation that will guide you in prioritizing each big rock. This powerful tool, embraced by Six Sigma philosophies, has personally helped me make career choices and balance multiple projects at once. A sample matrix is provided in the practice exercises section at the back of this book.

A practical example of prioritizing big rocks is provided by a colleague of mine, Lila, who manages multiple projects at a time and maintains a master list of all the tasks she has to do. She includes sub-items that link to the larger goal. (If you're like me, such a list is too long to fit on one piece of paper, so keeping the list up to date electronically using software such as Microsoft Outlook's Tasks feature or even just a word processing program works best.) Every week, Lila looks ahead in her calendar and updates the master list. Each day, using her priority criteria, she breaks down her task list and decides on the priority items to be accomplished that day (the big rocks). Lila focuses on doing these things first, before opening mail or responding to calls and emails (the gravel and sand). She thereby makes sure that, no matter what happens, these tasks get done.

Sound easy? Yes, it may *sound* simple, but being a leader is a demanding balancing act, especially for those who have families or are caregivers for an aging parent or those who are going through times of transition. Personal, family or health issues can drain a person's energy—literally—as can looking for a new job, starting a new job or moving. Even thinking about what lies ahead, whether known or unknown, may be physically and emotionally daunting. Furthermore, our day-to-day reality is that we live in an

> We need to strive for excellence, not perfection. Excellence tolerates mistakes, perfection doesn't.

overscheduled and "strive to be busy" culture. This may be why more people are medicated for depression today than at any other time in history. Many of these people may be perceived as confident, as having it all together, when they're actually fighting a battle against stress and burnout, which often leads to anxiety and depression.

After first attempting Lila's technique, I became frustrated. Every time I looked at my to-do list, I felt a sense of anxiety that made me feel resentful toward the company I was working for because of the time I had to put in. The list got increasingly longer, and I didn't have time to complete tasks to shorten it. I asked Lila, "Why does this work for you and not for me?" Lila passed on some empowering wisdom: "It's not just about the things you add to the list. It's also about the things you cross off the list. We are human *be*ings, not human *do*ings." Lila continued, "We need to strive for excellence, not perfection. The difference between excellence and perfection is that excellence tolerates mistakes and not getting everything done. Perfection doesn't."

Lila then went on to explain that she continuously re-evaluates what is realistic as well as really important, and thus often crosses things off the list even if they haven't been completed. This carves out time for the more important things. I realized that I had conjured up unrealistic expectations for myself, which was one of the reasons I felt so overwhelmed by my to-do list. I had put too many items on it. I now keep a sticky note on the front of my computer as a reminder. It reads, "The main thing is to keep the main thing the main thing." Once you have prioritized the big rocks, the next step is to break them down.

→ Excellence not perfection!

Breaking Down the Big Rocks into Stones

Lifting a tree may seem impossible, but if you take a saw and cut the tree into smaller pieces, lifting each piece is manageable. Likewise, seeing the goal as reading one chapter is less overwhelming than finishing the whole book. Furthermore, you are more likely to start and less likely to procrastinate when the goal is manageable.

Take for example Herb Kelleher, founder of Southwest Airlines. His motto was "Think small and act small, and we'll get bigger. Think big, be complacent, be cocky, and we'll get smaller." Herb understood and successfully applied the Five Seconds at a Time technique. He believed overwhelming people could lead to complacency, so he avoided it by rejecting the idea of long-range planning and instead focused on breaking strategic plans into six-month intervals. If you're stuck to a long-term plan, it's easy to lose agility of thought and action. In an interview for *Fortune* magazine, Herb stated, "We say do strategic planning, define what you are and then get back together soon to define whether you need to change that . . . because this plan about what we're going to do ten years from now will almost certainly be invalidated in the next six months."[6]

You will be relieved to hear of Little's Law, which shows that less is actually more. This practical law, proved mathematically in 1961 by John Little, former professor at MIT's Sloan School of Management, demonstrates that it is most effective to place a strong focus on smaller, staggered segments. Have you ever been faced with many large tasks and found yourself heading off in all directions, not completing any of them? When there are an infinite number of things you could be doing, you're at risk of falling into the trap of starting one task and then getting pulled to another faster than you can change your focus. Starting a new project ahead of schedule does not necessarily mean it will be finished sooner if you already have multiple projects on the go. Little's Law shows that if there are no increases in resources, it is better to reduce the number of projects at a given time. Why? Projects don't begin to pay off until they are complete. It is better to reap the savings or benefits of three completed projects than to have ten projects started and the completion time of those first three lengthened. Also, having multiple projects on the go can often burn us out, thus delaying the completion even further. Morale and productivity are much higher when people see the results of their efforts sooner and use the energy produced from those results to move on to the next project.

Many consulting companies and factories apply Little's Law. For example, one company writes, "Reducing work in process [WIP] may require some counterintuitive actions. Among these are temporarily pulling projects or orders out of the workflow and setting them aside. With the resulting decline in WIP, cycle time [completion time] drops and the remaining projects get done better and faster. So much so that projects originally pulled out of the workflow can then be reinserted, often being completed on or before the original planned target date. In other words, by stopping work on a project, it gets done faster."[7]

Furthermore, each time you switch from one task to another, a refocusing cost is incurred. In fact, a 2007 study revealed that Microsoft workers took, "on average, fifteen minutes to return to serious mental tasks, such as writing reports or computer code after responding to incoming email or instant messages."[8]

Try dividing large projects into smaller parts. For example, instead of blocking the entire day to work on a project, reserve five one-hour blocks of time to work on specific tasks. If you are interrupted, it will be much easier to refocus on the individual task you were working on than to return to the project as a whole. After all, as Little's Law proves, your productivity will improve if you prioritize projects and then break them into manageable, focused tasks.

The exercise of prioritizing and subdividing tasks has to be done every day to be effective. It will take a little longer the first time, but once you get a feel for these practices, they become habits. Be flexible. A high priority goal set yesterday may require recalibrating as medium priority today if something has come up that demands your immediate attention. Over time, by focusing proactively on the big rocks, you will find that urgent situations happen less often. Lila, for example, found that when she spent more quality time with her son (big rock), his temper tantrums decreased. Likewise, when Lila spent more time coaching her employees (big rock), their ability to solve problems independently increased.

> Instead of blocking the entire day to work on a project, reserve five one-hour blocks of time to work on specific tasks.

The art of breaking things down into smaller pieces will have a profound impact on your life. As you step back, also make sure that the things you are breaking down are real-istic in the first place. This is especially important for Type A personalities. I continuously have to re-evaluate the expecta-tions and pressures I put on myself and determine what is realistic and what isn't. Doing this helps me set better pri-orities and reminds me of the big rocks. The reality is that you can't do it all. Finding balance means accepting that you won't get *everything* done.

SETTING YOUR PRIORITIES

BRAINSTORM the big rocks, or priorities, for the week ahead. Big rocks could relate to your job, volunteer work, family, health or specific projects. It may help to write all your to-dos down first and then determine which rocks are the biggest.

ORGANIZE these big rocks into priority sequence if not all of them will fit into the "jar" this week.

BREAK DOWN each rock into stones, thus creating a list of tasks to accomplish.

ESTABLISH TIMELINES for the items on this list, focusing on what needs to be completed by the end of the week; from there, determine what needs to get done each day. Highlight items that need to be done today.

Just as important as breaking down projects into tasks is setting realistic goals and timelines. You are the best judge of what is realistic for you and what you can accomplish. The following diagram[9] illustrates what happens to performance and productivity when we allow ourselves to have unrealistic goals.

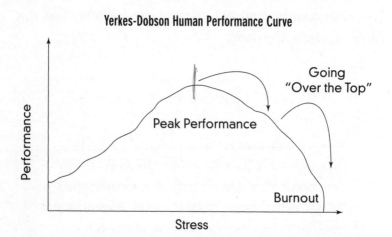

Yerkes-Dobson Human Performance Curve

The emotional and physical effects of stress often take a toll on both our bodies and our families, thus creating a negative spiral. The Five Seconds at a Time principles of prioritizing and re-evaluating priorities will help you stay at the top of the peak performance curve. Recognize that staying there may require that you ask for help, extend your timeline, change your goal or simply say "no." Stress isn't all bad, however. Optimal stress levels can enable us to move toward accomplishing our goals. The optimal level of stress for performance output is different for everyone since we each have a unique chemistry and makeup. We can find this optimal level through trial and error and reflection.

A popular and effective tool used by many successful organizations to break down the components of goals is the "SMART" technique, which states that goals should be Specific, Measurable, Achievable, Rewarded and Time-limited:

- Specific: The goal should name a specific desirable outcome. Have you identified what is within and outside of the scope of this goal?
- Measurable: The goal should produce quantifiable results. What measures will tell you when the goal has been reached? Financial savings, successful survey results, feedback from others?
- Achievable: The goal should be realistic. Do you have the resources needed to accomplish this goal?
- Rewarded: Accomplishing the goal should have clear benefits. What are the benefits of achieving this goal? What ways will you personally reward yourself once you've reached the goal?
- Time-limited: The goal should have a specific, realistic date of completion assigned to it. What timelines have you set for accomplishing the goal?

Acknowledging When Stepping Stones Are Accomplished and Rewarding Yourself

As important as earlier steps is the need to step back once each segment of the goal is completed and rejoice in what you have accomplished. Often, in our drive to perform, we forget to reflect on and celebrate our wins. Celebrations should be frequent and involve doing something that gives you pure joy and restores your energy, perhaps going to your favourite class at the gym, picking up a new book, taking a rejuvenating nap or socializing with friends. Your mind and body need the reward of rest and recharging to function optimally.

New York Times bestseller *The Power of Full Engagement* connects the patterns of athletic accomplishment to business accomplishment. Professional athletic coaches have discovered that what athletes do during their recovery periods (breathing patterns, positive self-talk, eye focus) determines how successfully they perform. The authors, Jim Loehr and Tony Schwartz, recommend that we "live like a sprinter . . . to break life down into a series of manageable intervals consistent with our own physiological needs and with the periodic rhythms of nature. . . . We, too, must learn to live our own lives as a series of sprints— fully engaging for periods of time, and then fully disengaging and seeking renewal before jumping back into the fray to face whatever challenges confront us."[10]

Building in rest periods and rewards is a proven way to segment each component of the goal, and it is integral to making the end point feel realistic. Celebration is not slacking off. Celebration drives recovery, renewal and future energy.

Sometimes in life, cascading series of challenging events occur, and you know things may not improve for a long time. Take, for example, the 2008 financial downturn in the markets and the economy that started in the United States and then rippled around the world. Employees were laid off, bonuses were halted, salary increases were frozen, and pensions eroded. Some surely faced a long period of depression. It is especially important to recognize and celebrate wins during these prolonged periods of challenge. Celebration could be as simple as mentally acknowledging positive situations or journaling things for which you are thankful. The night I was stranded on the mountain seemed to last an eternity. I was not entirely certain that I would see the rising sun again. But I celebrated each five-second breath I was granted by thanking God and consciously feeling grateful. Had I not done this, I believe I would not have survived the staggering task ahead of me.

In the practice exercises section at the back of this book, I have given an example of a situation in which an overwhelmed person faced with the challenges of both moving and starting a new full-time job can successfully use the stepping back techniques to accomplish what first seemed impossible.

Stepping Forward by Strengthening Your Inner Leadership

After implementing the Five Seconds at a Time technique to step back from my overwhelming and paralyzing feelings on the mountain, I "stepped forward" by drawing on qualities that have made me an effective leader in both my personal and professional life. Before I stepped off a rock, I mentally rehearsed which specific finger of ice immediately in front of me would be the landing point of the second-from-front spike of my *right* boot. I then *envisioned* precisely where the second-from-front spike on my *left* boot would land before I took action and stepped off the rock. I repeatedly visualized and mentally rehearsed a sequence of steps before I lifted my eyes to the desired rock target, all the while calling out to God for help and then simply stepping out in faith. I used *intuition* to listen to my body and took short rests to recover physically and mentally when necessary. During these breaks, I breathed deeply and deliberately chose to *focus on positive thoughts,* which included prayer and *trust that I would be saved.* After I reached the interim rock, cracked off the ice and gratefully stepped onto it, I repeated that painstaking step-by-step process until I arrived at the hut. At the hut, I had to initiate a series of *corrective actions* in order to survive since I had incorrectly assumed that the hut would provide warm shelter and a means of signalling for help.

The leadership techniques that saved my life can be used by others who also face seemingly impossible tasks. I would like to highlight that we often associate the word *leader* with a person in a position of authority and importance; however, one doesn't need to occupy a certain position to demonstrate leadership skills. Leadership is a state of mind; it is a disposition, not a position. It is a thought choice, not a title. Parents, students, violinists and bricklayers alike may demonstrate leadership daily and can apply leadership techniques to help them get through life's challenges. We step forward by managing ourselves through our challenges and by strengthening our inner leadership.

My mountaintop experience taught me that at the climax of crisis and panic, it is difficult to think beyond the immediate moment. I had to literally use five-second intervals to fight through the impossible, and it was only after I had stepped

> Leadership is a state of mind; it is a disposition, not a position.

back that I could step forward. Vision, Intuition, Positive Thought Choice, Faith and Action, and Correction are the habits that strengthened my inner leadership ability and the principles that helped me step forward. These five sequential principles, or "stepping stones," can guide you through the overwhelming toward accomplishing your big rocks.

THE FIVE STEPPING STONES

VISION: Mentally rehearse each step and envision what success looks like.

INTUITION: Pause to listen inwardly, reflect and regroup. Sometimes intuition precedes vision, faith or correction.

POSITIVE THOUGHT CHOICE: Choose thoughts that have the power to fuel your emotions into productive and impactful actions.

FAITH AND ACTION: Step out into action. This often involves stepping outside your comfort zone to attempt something new.

CORRECTION: Realign for future success.

I had learned these inner leadership principles one step at a time prior to my experience on Mount Ruapehu. I believe each stepping stone is necessary for leaders to achieve seemingly impossible goals. Vision, Intuition, Positive Thought Choice, Faith and Action, and Correction may sound simple, but do not become overwhelmed by trying to implement them all at once. Step back using the Five Seconds at a Time technique to break down each individual principle, and you will find it easier to begin to naturally apply the habits to your everyday life.

It is unrealistic to expect to accomplish the impossible alone, which makes developing leadership skills essential, since you will need the support and guidance of people who believe in you, believe in your vision and believe in your ability to accomplish the challenge. They must know that when you make a mistake, you will take personal ownership and act to correct it. These people must trust you as a leader and witness you living by your values. People want to be led, not managed. The only person we manage is ourselves—that's self-discipline. And only when we have self-discipline can we influence and lead other people. As Mahatma Gandhi taught, "as human beings, our greatness lies not so much in being able to remake the world . . . as in being able to remake ourselves."

Most important is the support of those who know you best— your family and closest friends—which means that demonstrating integrity and leadership at home is even more important than demonstrating it in the office. This leads me to another important point: Stepping stones need to be firmly placed on a strong foundation in order for them to be supported. Habit, authenticity and integrity are the bedrock needed to support you as you work through meeting life's challenges and accomplishing your goals. It is not enough to understand what the five stepping stones are; to reach the big rock, they need to be rooted in your *habits. Authentic leadership* requires that you not simply "turn on" the habit when it's convenient or when you are trying to impress someone. Authentic leadership involves continuously and genuinely walking your talk while working to achieve your goals. A wise person "builds a house on solid rock. Though the rain comes in torrents and the flood-waters rise and the winds beat against the house, it won't collapse, because it is built on bedrock" (Matthew 7:24–25, NLT). I discuss both habit and authentic leadership further in later chapters.

In times of crisis, companies can use the Five Seconds approach effectively. The year 2008 was challenging for many food manufacturing companies due to the *bacterium listeria* monocytogenes being found in several foods. Tragically, Maple Leaf Foods products were linked to several illnesses and losses of life. The company voluntarily recalled more than 190 products, temporarily shut down one of its Toronto meat processing facilities and settled class-action lawsuits for $27 million.[11]

Navigating a sea of complexity, uncertainy and fear, the whole management team came together to validate the facts as a group, discuss how to pinpoint the source, brainstorm their next steps and determine the resources they needed during the product recall. "This prioritizing and breaking down of next steps was essential before we could move forward into action," according to human resources manager Gary Gabet. "During a crisis, it is important to remember that you are not an island. Reaching out to others for support is essential. There was no finger pointing. We worked together as one and encouraged each other. The crisis itself, combined with working day and night, put both an emotional and physical toll on everyone.

We brought in professional counsellors so people could step back, talk about and process their experiences."[12]

During the product recall, quality manager Juan Alvarez had hundreds of things on his mind, both personally and professionally, but coped by taking time to step back from his work for greater perspective. "You can't just dive into activities and go-go-go without thinking and planning first, especially when other people are looking to you for direction. It simply won't work. I make a point of reflecting and planning before I start moving. Worrying only adds clutter. I have a personal practice of de-cluttering my mind with 5S so that I can step forward to face daily challenges and be able to focus on what's really important." 5S is a Japanese system used to create a disciplined and well-ordered physical environment because disorganized people often spend time searching for misplaced papers, files or emails, which can lead to decreased productivity. Juan points out that physical clutter also attracts the attention of the subconscious mind, forcing your mind to work harder than it needs to.

THE 5S SYSTEM

SORT. First, write down all the things on your mind and then sort them into groups: urgent, important and non-important. Then remove unnecessary items.

SET PRIORITIES so you can concentrate on what you want your mind to do first. Remove everything from your mind that you don't need and put back what you do need. If it's on paper, in a place that can be easily reached, you won't forget and thus don't need to think about it now.

SHINE your mind by engaging in positive thoughts.

STANDARDIZE by incorporating items into one centralized spot like a daybook with a calendar and task list.

SUSTAIN by repeating this practice at the beginning of every day and when transitioning from work to home to help focus on work while at work and on home while at home.

Maple Leaf Foods settled lawsuits out of court quickly and fairly and is striving to be a world leader in food safety. Their transparency and focus on consumers' health resulted in a successful recovery with consumer brand confidence rising to 91 per cent.

So the question posed at the beginning of this chapter, "How do you eat an elephant?" can now be answered simply: "One mouthful at a time!" The Five Seconds at a Time technique is like eating the elephant. Taking one day at a time is a specific habit that will pay huge dividends, especially for those with significant leadership responsibilities. I believe this lesson to be so vital that I consciously set out to create the answer to the elephant question as an automatic response to *any* problem situation. I am now convinced that the most successful way to solve a problem is to focus on the goal and take one step after the other. My mountaintop experience has given me a bone-marrow-deep appreciation for the Chinese proverb "A journey of a thousand miles begins with a single step." This proverb can serve as a guiding principle for any and every challenge.

Take Five Seconds

Points to Ponder
Stepping back to gain a broader perspective is a key ingredient of Five Seconds at a Time.

Every challenge can be broken down into manageable bites.

Quotes to Remember
"In three words I can sum up everything I've learned about life: It goes on." —*Robert Frost*

"I am not discouraged, because every wrong attempt discarded is another step forward."
—*Thomas A. Edison*

"Bite off more than you can chew, then chew it."
—*Ella Williams*

Questions to Consider
The sticky note I keep on my personal computer reads, "The main thing is to keep the main thing the main thing." What distracts you from your priorities? How can you keep your priorities (big rocks) the main focus in your life?

3

FOCUS ON THE ROCKS
VISION

"The journey is what matters. Once committed to a Vision, we are in a position to act. In striving to achieve our desire, being tested by what transpires and growing as a result, we travel a road that will add our unique cycle to history."
—*John Varney*

Upon reflection, I realized that vision had helped save my life on Mount Ruapehu. I now rejoice in having been familiar with envisioning techniques and having practised them in both my personal and professional life prior to ascending the mountain. In a time of crisis, I instinctually applied this skill.

It is crucial that the leadership stepping stones described in this text be practised with awareness in day-to-day life so they become second nature and easy to access during challenging

Visualization + self talk.

times. It would be difficult to call on these principles for the first time during a crisis situation.

Creating images of success (of the sun rising and a helicopter coming to rescue me) in my head was an envisioning exercise that I believe significantly contributed to my survival (my big rock). As I stood on a de-iced rock, I not only painted an extremely detailed picture of how and where each spike on both boots would land on the glassy surface but also rehearsed the envisioned sequence of steps at least ten times before venturing from the security of the rock. Knowing that once I stepped from the safety of my rock I could not go back, I chose to rehearse it so well visually that once I set out, I believed I *was* going to make it to the next protruding rock I had mentally selected. It is important to note that once I had taken those first three crucial steps, I lifted my eyes to the rock I was aiming at de-icing next and kept *my sights on that vision,* not looking down.

Keep Your Sights on Where You're Headed

One of my favourite parables is set in medieval Italy, where a visitor strolling through town stumbles upon a man cutting stone. The curious traveller asks, "What are you working on?" The man responds, "Cutting stone." The visitor continues on his walk and sees another man doing the same. Again the visitor asks, "What are you working on?" The man replies, "I'm building a wall." A few hours later, the traveller happens upon a third stonecutter and asks the same question, to which the reply is, "I'm building a cathedral."

Management consultant Peter Drucker uses this story to illustrate the power of vision. A purposeful outcome attached to a vision contributes to its successful fulfillment. Envisioning what success looks like and speaking enthusiastically about it will help you fulfill your own goals. What is the big picture behind the work you do? Is it serving a customer, teaching others, saving money? Use a vibrant big-picture vision to fuel you as you look forward to your desired future state. Dr. Kerry Spackman, world-renowned neuroscientist and coach of many elite athletes affirms that "making goals come alive" is what distinguishes Olympic champions. "Their goals are that much more real and vibrant than anyone else's. . . . Their goals never fade even when the going gets really, *really* tough. They still have belief and can find one more ounce of energy to keep on going in impossible situations."[13]

We see what we choose to and tend to find what we look for. The things we give attention to are amplified; therefore, what we focus on is crucial. Many mothers describe having focused on the vision of the baby while breathing their way through labour and delivery. Farmers know that they cannot look down and expect to plow straight. Similarly, whereas mountain climbers must focus on the rocks, mountain bikers quickly learn that when on a narrow trail, if they look at the loose rocks, they will likely hit them, so they focus on the spaces between the rocks, and that's where they ride. RCMP officers have reported that, generally, when a driver sees a potential accident forming on the highway, the natural tendency is to turn the wheels *toward* the accident. It is our imagination that creates the reality—our imagined crash facilitates the real one. Young Drivers of Canada (a driver's licence training centre) teaches drivers that when they are driving at speed on a straight stretch of highway, they should *build strengths not weakness!*

look ahead to the point down the road where they want to arrive—never down at the flashing yellow stripes.

After my Mount Ruapehu experience, I was rescued from near-certain death a second time. On June 25, 2009, while travelling home late at night with my wife, Mary Lynn, I was momentarily blinded by a pair of huge headlights that appeared unexpectedly right in front of me. I was travelling full speed on a two-lane highway, and the oncoming truck had moved into my lane to pass a smaller vehicle. I recall that, while initially dazed and caught in the headlights of the truck barrelling toward me, I instantly implemented my training to focus on where I wanted to go, not where I didn't want to go. So I wrenched the steering wheel toward the desired and envisioned place of safety—the shoulder. We skidded for several yards as the rush of wind caused by the speeding truck shook us.

Mary Lynn and I sat speechless for several minutes as the Grim Reaper moved on. (The driver did not stop, so might have been either drunk or asleep at the wheel.) We are alive because of my habit to focus on what I want, not on what I don't.

Similarly, in my consulting work and management workshops, I stress the importance of building on strengths, not weaknesses. If a manager or parent, for example, focuses on the weaknesses of those in his or her "care," those weaknesses, ironically, will be amplified.

Imagine in Advance

One application of envisioning is keeping your sights on the point at which you want to arrive. Another is imagining in advance. Having become second nature to successful leaders, this technique is far from casual daydreaming. Peak performers practise it repeatedly and with great concentration. Sports stars create mental images of the exact movements they want to make in their game. Boston Celtics' star player and later coach Bill Russell wrote in his book *Second Wind*, "I was sitting there with my eyes closed, watching plays in my head. I was in my own private basketball laboratory, making mental blueprints for myself."

Liu Chi Kung placed second to Van Cliburn in the 1958 Tchaikovsky Competition and was imprisoned a year later during the cultural revolution in China. For the seven years he was held in prison, he was denied the use of a piano; however, on a daily basis he practised envisioning techniques. After he was released, his concerts were even better than they'd been before. Reporters asked Liu how this was possible, and he told them, "I practised every day. I rehearsed every piece I had ever played, note by note, in my head."[14]

Similarly, martial artists rehearse *kata* (patterns of moves) to achieve what is called *mushin*, or "mind of no mind." This is the single trait most characteristic of skilled martial artists. Mind of no mind is the mental state achieved once the *kata* are so engrained and second nature to the body that the martial artist does not have to think before performing them. The true martial artist can perform action without thought. This concept can take many years of hard training to achieve and is learned only through practice and repetition. Seasoned instructors teach that practising in the mind once is more effective than physically performing the *kata* ten times over.

Research has shown that imagined events imprinted in the

mind can be recorded by the brain and central nervous system as memories. With practice and repetition, one's imaginings can become so vivid as to be indistinguishable from one's actual memories. Medical research reports positive findings from an imagery program done with patients diagnosed with medically incurable cancer. Those who chose to regularly see and feel their body parts heal or imagined themselves totally recovered were positively affected: 41 per cent showed improvement, and 22 per cent experienced total remission.[15] This suggests that the practice of imagining in advance enhances the immune system. Biofeedback and placebo research also provide evidence of the benefits of imagery.[16]

My mountain experience confirmed for me the idea that because our thinking and perception is selective, our reality actually becomes what we choose to perceive, our choice of focus. That means we actually create our own reality! The power of vision, therefore, is central to our lives. This is surely what King Solomon meant when he said, "Without vision, people perish." My story is a testament to this truth.

Think Possibility versus Probability

The essential nature of visions is that they are about possibilities and desired futures. They are therefore ideals, standards of excellence and expressions of optimism and hope. The leader who adopts a mode of thinking based on visions opens him- or herself up to considering possibilities, not simply probabilities. My envisioning techniques (plus my conviction that without vision I would have perished) were the foundation for my considering possibilities, not just probabilities. The reality is that probabilities are based upon evidence strong

possibilities + probabilities

enough to establish presumption. The real power of possibilities is that they need not be based on presumption. Any new venture begins with *possibility thinking*, not probability thinking. The successful leader operates from the assumption that anything is possible. Like entrepreneurs, leaders focus on *possibility thinking*; its power is what sustains them through difficult times.

probability vs. possibility!

> Any new venture begins with possibility thinking, not probability thinking.

As T.E. Lawrence wrote in *Seven Pillars of Wisdom*, "All men dream: but not equally. Those who dream by night in the dusty recesses of their minds wake in the day to find that it was vanity: but the dreamers of the day are dangerous men, for they may act their dreams with open eyes, to make it possible."

Goals versus Visions

In *Peak Performers*, Charles Garfield suggests that leaders of outstanding nature always have a vision and are driven by a sense of mission. It is this mission that kindles the imagination and motivates people to increased levels of achievement over long spans of time. Anybody can get excited about something momentarily, but what happens when the tent falls and the circus moves on? Vision must be present to ensure that a commitment remains. A living vision that exists in our hearts, thoughts and actions inspires our energy.

Warren Bennis, one of today's authorities on leadership,

has spent the past fifteen years interviewing top leaders and CEOs. In the course of his research, a theme emerged about these leaders and about the kind of leadership that will be necessary to forge the future. While leaders come in every size, shape and disposition, there are at least two ingredients common to all: a guiding purpose and an overarching vision. Leaders are more than goal directed; they are vision directed.

It is worth noting that I have chosen the word *vision* over *mission* or simply *goals* because a vision, as in its linguistic definition, can be *pictured*—it has substance, form and colour. Research suggests that 78 per cent of the information most people absorb is visual. Our eyes are the portals to our minds. Leaders not only understand the power of vision but use it to attract others to their dream. John Sculley, former chair of Apple Computers, inspired followership with his dream. In 1987, he stated, "Don't give people goals; tell them which way to go. We want people to reach ideas they haven't dreamed of yet. Unlike most corporations, we don't so much try to define our identity; we try to make it recognizable—not too concrete. So we talk endlessly—and aphoristically—about what we do: 'We build people, not computers' or 'The best way to predict the future is to invent it.' Most corporate planners decide where the company should go in the next year or two by peering into the company's past and making judgments and extrapolations based on their experiences. We ask ourselves, What will 1992 be like? We create in our minds a portrait of the economy, our industry and our company. Then we move back into the present, envisioning what we have to do to get to the future."

The literature on vision sometimes confuses it with mission. Vision is the future desired state. Mission, on the other hand, is the means by which the vision is realized—for example, the reason a person, department, team or organization exists. My mountain experience has prompted me to ask some tough questions about God's reasoning: Why was I rescued? Why am I still here? What's my purpose and life's work?

Upon reflection of these deep philosophical questions, I've found a clear sense of mission (at least for my professional life) as the "unlocking of talents." My personal vision statement is "heaven on earth." Vision moves us toward what we want, rather than toward what we do not want. It draws us forward and takes us beyond obstacles. Vision provides motivation. On Mount Ruapehu, envisioning survival and safety inspired me to keep going and saved my life. Vision will enhance your leadership success and will help you achieve your big rocks.

Vision and Followership

Although the theme of this book revolves primarily around achieving individual or personal visions, I would like to touch on larger organizational visions. In order to achieve corporate or political visions, you will need to create a followership of people who can help you. In his race for leadership of the Democrats, for example, President Barack Obama successfully created a powerful empire, even with a thin résumé of experience. He was able to articulate his vision for America with his outstanding command of language. He was also able to create a campaign vision that fulfilled an unmet need and answered the public's question, "What's in it for me?" Obama's vision of change appealed to those who were frustrated by the Bush administration.

Jeffrey Gandz, Ivey School of Business professor and executive development program director, has researched vision extensively and identified four elements of compelling vision that are needed to create effective followership.

THE FOUR CS OF A COMPELLING VISION

CONTENT that meets followers' wants and fulfils previously unmet needs.

CONTEXT that makes the vision compelling. The vision must be delivered at an appropriate time and place so that followers will receive the message well.

CREDIBILITY, which evolves from both the visionary and the vision. The vision must contain evidence-based solutions, and the visionary must be charismatic.

COLLABORATION with those engaged in creating the vision. Collaboration and a shared vision inspire commitment, as they integrate individuals' own personal visions and empower collaborators because the vision belongs to them, too. Potential collaborators will turn away from leaders who are perceived as manipulative.

Jeff's *Peanuts* cartoon analogy may make you smile. Lucy is teaching Charlie Brown about the concept of vision. "Charlie Brown, life is like a deck chair on a cruise ship. Passengers open up these canvas deck chairs so they can sit in the sun. Some people place their chairs facing the rear of the ship so they can see where they've been. Other people face their chairs forward—they want to see where they're going. On the cruise ship of life, which way is your deck chair facing?" Charlie Brown in a confused response utters, "I've never been able to get one unfolded."[17]

Vision is facing forward to see where you are going. Intuition involves facing backward to reflect on life, where you have been, how you felt and what you learned from your past actions so that you can apply this to the present. When you consider that the Latin root of *intuition* means to look at, the connection between intuition and vision is clear. And since vision may spring from intuition, vision may not always be the first step in goal accomplishment. In the next chapter, we will discuss how intuition can act as a "sound check" to our visions.

Take Five Seconds

Points to Ponder
An obstacle is what you see when you take your sights off the vision.

Your vision is your product. It wasn't raining when Noah built the ark.

Quotes to Remember
"The future belongs to those who believe in the beauty of their dreams." —*Eleanor Roosevelt*

"Of the hundreds of vision statements I have heard, I cannot think of one that did not in some way call for love, compassion or teamwork." —*Peter Block*

"Before you begin a thing, remind yourself that difficulties and delays quite impossible to foresee are ahead. . . . You can only see one thing clearly and that is your goal. Form a mental vision of that and cling to it through thick and thin."
                                        —*Kathleen Norris*

Question to Consider
Do I alternate the position of my chair to achieve a balance of vision and reflective thought?

4

LEAVE YOUR THINKING MIND BEHIND
INTUITION

"Intuition is the ability to solve problems with insufficient data."
—Joel Barker

When I have been most effective, it is invariably because I have listened to my inner voice. I openly acknowledge intuition as a key reason for my survival on Mount Ruapehu. After failing to find Bruce by descending the mountain, I vividly remember collapsing on a de-iced rock in both physical and emotional despair. When an incoming cloud blocked my view, I was faced with an agonizing choice: Should I continue my descent and search? Or should I attempt to climb back up in hopes of finding a phone or some other means of help in the hut on the peak? The daylight was beginning to fade, and I feared getting lost in the bush if I kept heading down. My mind did not seem capable of making a rational decision at that point of exhaustion, confusion and inner turmoil—which is when my intuition kicked in and prompted me to climb back up, a decision that I believe has influenced my life ever since.

In hindsight, and in stepping back, which is the easiest way to see the workings of the still, quiet inner voice, I am convinced that had I not followed my intuitive hunch to climb up, I would not have been blessed with the gift of such a profound mountaintop experience; I would not have been found by the rescue party (being lost in the bush would have made this virtually impossible); I may not have met and married my beloved wife, Mary Lynn; and you would not be reading this book.

Although intuition is very important for leaders, our modern Western culture often does not acknowledge its validity, regarding it as too "soft" or mystical a process to accept. While we respect, honour and develop the rational aspects of our nature, we discard and discount the intuitive side. As a nonlogical activity, intuition is extremely difficult to study, explain and quantify. To heighten your understanding of it, I will explore how intuition relates to our instinct, spirit and emotion.

The Relationship between Intuition and Instinct

The term *instinct* is often used interchangeably with *intuition*, but in reality instinct and intuition, while related, are very different. Animals live by their instinct, which naturally directs them to perform behaviours and acts necessary for them to survive both individually and as a species. As animals, human beings also have instinctual energies that prompt us toward self-preservation.

But in addition to instinct, we humans have intuition, a faculty that gives us a much broader spectrum of information, related not only to our survival but also to our growth, development, self-expression and higher purpose. Instinctual behaviour is usually similar among all members of a given species, whereas intuition seems to be fine-tuned to individual human needs.

The Relationship between Intuition and Spirit

The awe-inspiring interconnectedness of our bodies, minds and souls has strong implications for leaders. Success is largely determined by the degree to which these facets of our being are operating together. Intuition, which is associated with our spirit, has to be recognized and considered when developing our leadership abilities. As I became open to my own inner voice, I started to understand that there was something divine, true and pure about it.

Some Christians define intuition as the inner speaking of the Holy Spirit. Many pray that God will work through their intuition to lead and guide them down the right path. Others have described encounters similar to my experience in which intuition was "given" to them from an outside higher source, a source that lives within them and strengthens them.

The Relationship between Intuition and Emotion

The word *feeling* can be used to describe both our intuitive promptings and our emotions, making it particularly easy to confuse the two. Our intuitive feelings and our emotional feelings are different yet intimately connected. The Canadian Oxford Dictionary defines emotion as "a strong mental or instinctive feeling such as love, sorrow or fear." Intuition is defined as "the power of understanding situations or people's feelings immediately, without the need for conscious reasoning or study." In a sense, intuition underlies and can guide our emotions. On the flip side, when we shut out our emotions, it is much more difficult to connect with our intuition. The more we allow ourselves to be in touch with our emotional feelings and ask ourselves why we feel what we do, the easier it is to access our intuitive feelings.

Daniel Goleman, author of *Emotional Intelligence*, teaches that emotional intelligence matters more than IQ and, therefore, redefines what it means to be smart. Goleman's research concludes that "the key to sounder personal decision-making [is], in short, being attuned to our feelings"[18] and that "people with greater certainty about their feelings are better pilots of their lives, having a surer sense of how they really feel about personal decisions from whom to marry to what job to take."[19]

My personal leadership experiences have convinced me that my effectiveness as a leader is determined by the degree to which I am aware of my values, listen to my inner voice and demonstrate the self-discipline to make my actions congruent with both the values and inner voice. Once my behaviour is congruent with my values and the inner voice, my experience is that of what many writers simply call "flow." Intuition can be a powerful tool in working toward accomplishing your big rocks.

When to Think Rationally and When to Think Intuitively

Intuition resides beyond our own sensibilities and sensory perceptions. Fuzzy, imprecise, intuitive sensing is different from logic and seems to work only after crisis, information and serendipity have occurred. If you just sit around waiting for warm, enlightened feelings, you may be fired or even locked up. But when those inner impressions come after research, thought, introspection and a commitment to openness, you can enjoy a powerful, passionate, confirming experience.

In *Blink: The Power of Thinking without Thinking*, Malcolm Gladwell presents several research studies on both the powers and dangers of intuition. Gladwell cautions against using intuition solely as a crystal ball and warns that intuition can be inaccurate, especially when false stereotypes impede good judgment. However, his extensive research concludes that "on straightforward choices, deliberate analysis is best. When questions of personal choice start to get complicated—when we have to juggle many different variables—then our unconscious thought processes may be superior."[20]

Worthy of sharing from Gladwell's thesis is a thought-provoking example of how a military commander used intuition to make the seemingly impossible possible. In 2000, the Pentagon initiated the planning of a sophisticated and costly two-and-a-half-week war game to test U.S. military strategies as a dress rehearsal for war. Partnering with the United States Joint Forces Command (JFCOM), the Pentagon sought to prove that technology could give the military confidence and the ability to systematically understand the enemy. Paul Van Riper, a Vietnam War hero, was chosen to lead the enemy team. Van Riper had his work cut out for him as the Pentagon invested a quarter of a billion dollars on its own part in the war simulation. The Pentagon's team had every piece of intelligence imaginable available to it from sources ranging from military specialists and software experts to high-powered satellites and computer analytic systems. The Pentagon was shocked and dismayed when a surprise attack by Van Riper's team resulted in sixteen American ships being pummelled by the second day of war, thus ending the simulation. More than 20,000 American troops had been lost.

How did Van Riper's team accomplish the seemingly impossible when the Pentagon's team had every expert and costly resource at its fingertips? Van Riper had trained his troops to think quickly on their feet and to use their experience, judgment and intuition in a rough mental simulation before acting. In fact, Van Riper's military philosophy was the antithesis of the Pentagon's. He believed that war is messy and non-linear and that powerful technology does not guarantee success. Against the systematic, rational and analytic decision-making process that the Pentagon believed in, Van Riper felt that in the real heat of war, comparing all available options calmly and carefully took far too long and was too tough to accomplish. "In command but out of control" was Van Riper's training slogan,[21] meaning that he provided the high-level strategy but empowered the members of his team to use their own initiative and innovation to make it happen. "Allowing people to operate without having to explain themselves . . . enables rapid cognition,"[22] wrote Gladwell. Thus, business leaders are enabling intuitive thought when they delegate and empower others.

We often think that the more information we have, the

better off we are. Gladwell's point is that too much information can actually be harmful because it doesn't allow us to look at the situation holistically and apply our own judgment. Also, as we become inundated with information, we often confuse it with understanding. The Pentagon's team lost because it got caught up in all the information and in synthesizing that information. Gladwell believes that "successful decision making relies on a balance between deliberate and instinctive thinking."[23]

This calls to mind the golf lessons I had earlier this year. Derek, my instructor, encouraged me to take a practice shot and think through all of the body mechanics and club positioning. "When you approach the ball for the real shot," Derek wisely instructed, "forget about everything. Just hit the ball." I was amazed—it worked! When I thought too much, I couldn't hit the ball. When I left "my thinking mind behind," as Derek described it, my swing just flowed naturally. I now tap my club twice on the ground after my practice shot as a reminder to switch off my brain.

On the flip side of being inundated with too much information, leaders are often faced with the challenge of having to make a decision when not all information is available or when the possible solutions are merely various shades of grey. In these cases, too, intuition can be a true source of wisdom, and many leaders use it successfully. As Sigmund Freud put it, "When making a decision of minor importance, I have always found it advantageous to consider all the pros and cons. In vital matters, however, such as the choice of a mate or profession, the decision should come from the unconscious, from somewhere within ourselves."

Leaders often claim to follow their gut feelings when making decisions, meaning simply that they have an increased awareness of their inner process. Those who have attempted to recognize the significance of intuition generally report that it has guided them in their most important choices. For example, American poet and celebrated speaker Ralph Waldo Emerson was known to listen to his inner voice and go with it despite all voices to the contrary. General Colin Powell, former U.S. Secretary of State, shared the following leadership lesson: "Use the formula $P = 40$ to 70, in which P stands for the probability of success and the numbers indicate the percentage of information acquired. Once the information is in the 40 to 70 range, go with your gut."[24] In other words, don't wait until you have 100 per cent of the information before making a decision, because you hazard "analysis paralysis" and delayed action, which increases risk. On the flip side, it is dangerous to make an impulse decision when you have less than a 40 per cent chance of being right.

Similarly, in *The Power Principle: Influence with Honor,* Blaine Lee quotes a CEO who regularly taps into his own intuition for a gut check when making decisions: "When we face a crisis, I get all the data I can get; I get all the information I can collect that bears on the problem. Then I pay the price, by doing my homework, by researching everything I can that relates to the issue. At the same time I keep the door open to new, unforeseen options. Finally, I sit in my office, all alone, and push all of the documents away. Then . . . I don't know how to describe this other than I just *listen* on the inside. And if I get a tingly feeling on the back of my neck, I move ahead.

And if I don't get that tingly feeling on the back of my neck, I don't do it. This process has seldom failed me."[25]

The movie *Touching the Void* captures the true survival story of Joe Simpson as he descended the Siula Grande in Peru. Joe would not have survived had he not listened to an intuitive hunch. He broke several bones in his leg during his descent and fell into a deep and deadly crevasse. With no hope of his climbing partner being able to find or save him, Joe had to accomplish the seemingly impossible—get out of the ice hole into which he'd fallen and descend the rest of the steep terrain to get back to the base camp. Joe could see the sun beaming in above him; however, with his severely injured leg, he was not able to get out, despite trying every possible manoeuvre to hoist himself up. Below him, the crevasse had a dark steep opening. Joe's only two options were to continue trying to climb out and possibly die of exhaustion or to risk the uncertainty of descending further into the dark hole. His intuition told him to do the latter, a decision that saved his life. Although the descent into the unknown darkness was frightening, it eventually led to another opening out of the crevasse.

A leader's intuition often leads him or her down a very different path than initially expected. It can be easy to assume that we are making a mistake because things do not go as we planned or how we think they ought to. Our rational minds, for example, may think we should proceed in a logical way from point A to point B to point C, whereas our intuition may guide us to skip point B altogether and arrive at point C through the back door. Or, even more disconcertingly, we may never arrive at point C at all but at point Z, which we never consciously knew existed as an option. The rational mind is like a computer: It processes the input it receives and calculates logical conclusions based on that information. The intuitive mind, on the other hand, seems to have access to infinite supplies of information, including information we have not gathered directly through personal experience. It has the ability to tap into a greater storehouse of knowledge and wisdom than does the rational mind. Through our intuition, we have access to much more information than we have through our rational faculties. In the best possible way, our intuition prompts us as to where we need to go. Sometimes, however, we must let go of things to which we have become strongly attached but that are either no longer needed or unhealthy in our lives.

Many successful leaders tap into their intuition, using it as a sounding board, when they are inundated with too much information or when they need to validate a decision without having all of the necessary information. Successful leaders also use their intuition as a creative inlet for dreaming up a new idea or vision.

Intuition as a Source of Creativity

"Follow your nose" is the mission most scientists dream of being given. Neuroscientist Bruce McNaughton declares that formal business planning and regimented processes can stifle the brightest of minds. In a recent *Globe and Mail* article, he challenges, "Name me a major recent clinical or technological breakthrough in neuroscience, and I'll show that it has its foundation in curiosity-driven research by people that are mostly retired."[26] Mathematical physicist Neil Turok agrees that "if you look back in history, the greatest wealth has come when people are free to pursue their own ideas and aren't constrained by a predetermined agenda."[27]

Research scientists often follow a hunch about which line of experimentation will be most fruitful. The famous story of Edison dreaming of the light bulb is a powerful example of how intuition interweaves with science and how intuitive guidance can come through our dreams and be a source of powerful creativity. Edison was known to sit in a chair holding a ball in each hand while he closed his eyes and daydreamed. When he was about to fall asleep, his arms would relax and the balls would drop to the floor, waking him up. Immediately, he would write down what he was dreaming. This is how he retrieved many of his inventive ideas.

> Research scientists often follow a hunch about which line of experimentation will be most fruitful.

Also known to have been a daydreamer is Leonardo da Vinci. While da Vinci was working on the painting *The Last Supper*, his employer often caught him catnapping or drifting off in thought and was upset that the artist couldn't work more steadily. It is not a coincidence that Leonardo da Vinci wrote, "The greatest geniuses sometimes accomplish more when they work less. . . . It is a very good plan every now and then to go away and have a little relaxation. When you come back to the work, your judgment will be surer, since to remain constantly at work will cause you to lose the power of judgment."[28]

Take a moment to reflect on what you were doing when you came up with your best ideas. In his book *How to Think Like Leonardo da Vinci: Seven Steps to Genius Every Day,* Michael Gelb asked thousands of people, "When do you get your best ideas?" These were the most common answers: while walking in nature, while listening to music, while in the shower or while resting in bed. Gelb's study concluded that very few people get their best ideas while doing structured work. Interestingly, our most creative ideas often occur when the rational (left) side of the brain is relaxed and when we are not consciously trying to seek a solution. I, for example, came up with many of the ideas for this book while brushing my teeth. This is the beauty of intuition at work. It excites me that legendary people like Leonardo da Vinci created their success by using the Five Seconds at a Time approach of stepping back, refocusing and listening to what was going on inside of them.

How to Tap into Your Intuitive Self

To develop your intuitive abilities, you must begin to pay attention to what is going on inside, so that you can become aware of inner dialogues and catch them when they are happening or shortly afterward. As you become more aware of your inner process, you will begin to notice intuitive feelings as they pop up. You will then be able to deal with them more consciously.

> Intuition is seldom dramatic, grandiose or particularly mystical.

Keep in mind that although we often refer to our intuition as our "inner voice," it does not necessarily "speak" to us in words or even register as a defined feeling. Sometimes it may materialize as a kind of inner knowing about a particular topic or about a course of action. Or it may come to us in the form of energy, through which we sense that we are being moved in a certain direction or blocked from moving a certain way. Intuition is seldom dramatic, grandiose or particularly mystical. It is generally a very natural and normal instinct.

Here is a quick, simple exercise that can help you tap into your intuition. Close your eyes and take a deep breath, exhaling slowly. Notice what is on your mind. What have you been thinking about? Notice how your body is feeling. How are you feeling emotionally? Do you feel that you are more or less "in the flow," following your own energy, or do you feel stressed, conflicted or out of sorts? Take another deep breath, exhale slowly and let your awareness move into a deep place inside. Is there anything you need to pay attention to that would help you feel more connected to yourself? Any gut feeling of which you should be aware? Whether or not you perceive any specific information or awareness, enjoy a moment of rest before you carry on.

It doesn't matter too much if nothing happens for you when you do this exercise. Just taking a moment to be with yourself and to tune in to your inner process on a deeper level will be very healing and will help with developing your intuition. The exercise may also help you get more fully into the here and now. The more present and connected with ourselves we are, the more likely we are to notice and follow our intuitive feelings, and the more effective we are likely to be in whatever we do.

To master the technique of following your intuition accurately, you must try to act on what you believe to be your intuition and then see what the results are, taking the feedback that life gives you and learning from it. Notice whether following your inner prompts brings you a feeling of greater aliveness. Also notice whether times when you don't act on an intuitive feeling leave you with a feeling of depression, numbness or loss of energy. When I am not following the flow of my energy, life becomes a struggle—as if I were trying to swim upriver all the time.

Most often, when you are following your intuitive energy, you will feel as though you are "in the flow" of life. Things evolve smoothly and easily. Opportunities open up, and you feel as if you are in the right place at the right time doing the right thing. You may experience a sense of synchronicity with other people and events. You may even experience a profound awareness of a higher power at work in the situation because it may seem that no individual human could have orchestrated things so perfectly. Even if you are not a believer in God, what if you prayed for him to work through your intuitions to lead and guide you? You really have nothing to lose by experimenting. If you are an atheist, why not test your theory?

Discovering Your Strengths through Intuition

Almost everyone at some point questions what life is about and why he or she is here on earth. As you develop your intuition, you will begin to experience subtle changes, which may lead you to examine your life with new eyes. You may also find yourself guided toward discovering and fulfilling a higher purpose. That higher purpose quite literally necessitates the sharing of the natural gifts you have been given.

We each possess unique talents, strengths and gifts and are blessed with at least one thing we can do better than anyone else in the world. We are all walking miracles, engineered for success, designed for accomplishment and endowed with the seeds of absolute greatness. When we recognize and build on these and other strengths, we are in tune with the way in which we were created and are destined to realize our phenomenal potential.

As a leader, you must be able to lead from the *inside*. It is only when your behaviours are congruent with your values, beliefs and strengths that you can successfully gain followership and influence. *Intuition-centred leadership* requires listening to your inner voice, identifying gifts and (perhaps with considerable difficulty) sticking to what you do best and continually refining those talents. You cannot expect to reap the rewards of outstanding leadership unless you focus time and energy on developing your areas of brilliance.

Your intuition can help you to better understand your specific strengths. And once you understand your strengths, you can build your vision and work toward accomplishing goals that may have once seemed impossible. The following exercise represents an essential three-step approach to using your intuition to help you understand your strengths better.

Understanding Your Strengths

SPECIFY your areas of brilliance (gifts and talents). What do you do effortlessly? What activities enable you to lose a sense of time? What do others marvel at that you do easily? Which of your activities produces the greatest result (income or fulfillment)?

RECORD all the activities in which you engage in a typical week. I suggest you keep a pad beside you for a week and jot down each activity you engage in (at fifteen-minute intervals). This will clearly indicate how you spend your most precious gift (time).

CALCULATE the percentage of time during the week that you spend on your top three areas of brilliance.

Step back, pause and complete the above three steps now. As Socrates wisely said, "The unexamined life is not worth living."

Focusing on Your Strengths

Most likely, this exercise will provide you with a wake-up call! Your bottom-line income is directly related to the percentage of time you spend in your God-given areas of brilliance. Focusing on your strengths will help you make what once seemed impossible possible. When I first did this exercise, the data was so disturbing I immediately hired an assistant to do computer work, which I find time-consuming, difficult and frustrating. We must either delegate our areas of non-brilliance or stagnate. As founder of *Success Magazine* Orison Swett Marden said, "Every great man has become great, every successful man has succeeded, in proportion as he has confined his powers to one particular channel."

If you don't have the means to delegate, consider ways you can focus more on developing your natural strengths. For example, I have had colleagues who have taken ownership of their career paths by specifically getting involved in projects that showcased their strengths. At first, these were usually extra initiatives, beyond their normal work duties. However, in time, their value in the area became evident, and these types of projects started getting assigned to them more regularly, while other projects were shifted onto different team members. Spending time working only on your weaknesses simply results in your having strong weaknesses and keeps you in the mediocre category of leaders. Besides, it is an insult to your integrity to major in minors. Peter Drucker affirmed in the *Harvard Business Review,* "Only when you operate from strengths can you achieve true excellence . . . . One should waste as little effort as possible on improving areas of low competence. It takes far more energy and work to improve from incompetence to mediocrity than it takes to improve from first-rate performance to excellence."[29]

The wisdom to build on strengths can also be illustrated within most successful marriages. The expression "Opposites attract" certainly does have some validity. I don't enjoy cooking, nor am I gifted at it. However, I am particularly thorough as a sous-chef and clean-up person. Mary Lynn is an amazingly creative and talented cook, but she uses any and every pan or utensil within reach. If I did not contribute my own strength of systematic clearing and cleaning, we would not be able to invite guests to the dinner parties for which we have become well known.

The 80/20 Rule, which you probably already know, states that 20 per cent of your tasks (input) account for roughly 80 per cent of the value of the things you do (output). For example, 20 percent of your clients generate 80 percent of your sales. Out of 20 per cent of your activities, can you account for 80 per cent of the value of your work? Do you say no to invitations or requests to engage in activities or tasks for which you are not ideally suited? From now on, resolve to spend *more* of your time focusing on big rocks that contribute the greatest value and enable you to achieve the most important results. Of equal significance is the need for you to identify the activities in the bottom 80 per cent. These are time-consuming activities that contribute very little to the desired results. Resolve to delegate, downsize and drop as many of them as possible.

Listening to, trusting and acting on your intuitive inner guidance is an art. Like any other art or discipline, it requires a certain commitment. It is an ongoing process in which you will always be challenged to move to a deeper level of self-trust. For most of us, allowing our intuition to guide us is really a new way of life, very different from what we have been taught in the past. At times, it may feel uncomfortable or even frightening. If we have been conditioned to approach life entirely rationally, to follow certain rules or to do what we think other people want us to do, then beginning to follow our own inner sense of truth is a major paradigm shift. Learning to follow your intuition can feel at times like "living on the edge." In a way, it requires learning to live without the false sense of security that comes from attempting to control everything that happens. But as we follow our own inner guidance, wonderful things unfold for us, things that we may not even yet imagine. Gradually, we become less afraid and more comfortable with uncertainty. We can learn to enjoy not knowing. We can learn to move into the unknown with the confidence that we have a guiding force within us that is showing us the way.

You are miraculously unique and gifted. Your leadership must be based on the courage to follow your calling. The next chapter illuminates how your thought choices significantly affect your actions toward following that calling. Let's step onto the next rock.

Take Five Seconds

Point to Ponder

Intuition can lead us toward finding our unique strengths and purpose to achieve our goals and dreams (our big rocks).

Quotes to Remember

"You have to leave the city of your comfort and go into the wilderness of your intuition. What you'll discover will be wonderful. What you'll discover is yourself." —*Alan Alda*

"What I am actually saying is that we need to be willing to let our intuition guide us and then be willing to follow that guidance directly and fearlessly."
                                                    —*Shakti Gawain*

"The only real valuable thing is intuition."
                                                    —*Albert Einstein*

Questions to Consider

How can I fully tap into my intuition to aid in decision making and creative thinking? How does faith in God link to intuition? What can I do to strengthen the relationship between my intuition and my spirit?

5

FEED THE VOICE OF GOOD
POSITIVE THOUGHT CHOICE

"God gives us gifts wrapped up as problems.
The bigger the problem, the bigger the gift."
—*Ralph Waldo Emerson*

I miss Bruce more than words can say, so I can hardly fathom the despair my sister, Kathleen, has faced at his loss. Bruce's death will remain a mystery to me until my turn comes to join him and I better understand God's ultimate plan for all of us. Yet the day I lost Bruce and the night that followed also afforded me the most intense learning experience I have ever had and most likely ever will have. Turning this tragedy into a learning experience to share with others, deciding to heal and working to pass on something positive to honour Bruce are examples of how I chose my thoughts and attitudes toward the situation I found myself in. After all, leadership success is measured not so much by the position that one reaches in life but by the obstacles the leader has overcome, by his or her endeavours to succeed and by the way he or she has touched others along the way. I attempt daily to be better, not bitter.

Choosing Your Attitude

The principle of thought choice is of great importance and should perhaps be regarded as the fundamental determinant of leadership success. It is not our circumstances but our attitude toward them that makes us either great leaders or mediocre ones. We can choose our thoughts, and thus, we can choose our attitudes. A successful leader recognizes and teaches followers that attitude is so much more important than either skills or knowledge. Our perspective and mental paradigms are totally in our (and only our) control.

An exercise that I have used to generate overwhelming evidence of the critical importance of our attitudes involves asking participants to write down the characteristics that come to mind whenever they think of an outstanding (or ideal) leader. I then give a brief description of the well-documented and widely used classification system of human behaviour known as KSA. Human behaviour can be described as having knowledge (K), skill (S) or attitude (A) as its basis. When participants are asked to write either K, S or A beside each of the leadership characteristics they've listed, the percentages tend to average out to 2 per cent knowledge, 4 per cent skill and 94 per cent attitude. "Attitude" characteristics include perseverance, commitment, courage, optimism, gratefulness, confidence and hope. The conclusion is that attitude is not the most important thing; it's the only thing. Interestingly, the letters in *attitude* total 100 per cent when A=1, B=2, C=3 and so forth: 1 + 20 + 20 + 9 + 20 + 21 + 4 + 5 = 100 per cent!

My mountaintop experience certainly supports the hypothesis that attitude is a more critical quality than knowledge or skills combined and gives emphasis to the claim that successful leadership requires effective thought choice. I could have remained helplessly on the floorboards, shivering uncontrollably, but I chose to pull myself up. The thought "I can do all things through Christ who strengthens me," thankfully, was rooted within me. Such positive thoughts controlled my feelings, my attitude and, subsequently, my drive to survive. Although neither my faith nor my attitude made me feel any warmer in the bone-rattling cold, I chose to lift my spirits, to rekindle my hope and to hold on to my faith. I attribute my survival to my attitude, my faith, my positive thinking, the envisioning techniques I used and the *attitude of gratitude* I adopted.

So how can you control your attitude? By learning to control your thoughts.

The Power of Your Thoughts

Wilma Mankiller, who became the first female chief of the Cherokee Nation, was known to wear a necklace with two wolf-head figurines facing each other. In an interview, she was asked what the two wolves represented. Her finger on one face, Wilma answered, "This one represents the voice of good that is inside of me. And this one," she said, pointing to the other, "represents the voice of evil. They are always in an internal battle." "Which one is winning?" the interviewer asked. "The one I feed the most."[30]

Except for that conduct that springs from our basic natural instincts, all conscious behaviour is preceded by, and arises from, our thoughts. Voluntary thoughts not only reveal what you are but also predict what you will become. The power of thoughts is no secret to leaders throughout history. Charles Darwin, for example, stated, "The highest possible stage in moral culture is when we recognize that we ought to control our thoughts." Philosopher René Descartes said, "I think; therefore I am." And the Bible states, "For as he thinks in his heart, so is he" (Proverbs 23:7, NKJV) and "Whatever is true, whatever is noble, whatever is right, whatever is pure, whatever is lovely, whatever is admirable—if anything is excellent or praiseworthy—think about such things" (Philippians 4:8, NIV). What we put into our minds determines what comes out in our words and actions. Examine what you are putting into your mind through television, books, conversations, movies and magazines. You will reap what you sow, whether you like it or not. If you wish to reap a different harvest, you need to plant different seeds—and this refers to *mental seeds*, or seeds of thought. The notion of sowing and reaping ties into the law of cause and effect. *Thoughts are causes, and conditions are effects.* Your thoughts are the primary causes of the condition of your life. A good portion of what you are, or will ever be, is a result of the way you think. This is because people tend to act in a way consistent with what they are thinking most of the time. Thus, they eventually become what they think about. If you change the quality of your thinking, you change the quality of your life. "Your thoughts, vividly imagined and repeated, while charged with emotion become your reality."[31]

What do Abraham Lincoln, Walt Disney and Michael Jordan have in common? They all achieved the seemingly impossible after they had first failed miserably. Most important, their thoughts significantly affected their success. Born into poverty, Abraham Lincoln lost several elections, was bankrupt and suffered from a nervous breakdown before becoming one of the most remembered American presidents. One of Abraham's most well-known quotations is "Always bear in mind that your own resolution to succeed is more important than any other one thing."

Similarly, Walt Disney lauded the power of the mind when he stated, "When you believe in a thing, believe in it all the way, implicitly and unquestionably." This is the mindset that encouraged him to persevere in securing funding to develop Disneyland even after many setbacks.

Also, did you know that Michael Jordan was cut from his high school basketball team? It is no coincidence that he is known for saying, "Always turn a negative situation into a positive situation" and "You have to expect things of yourself before you can do them."

I enjoy using the following example in my seminar work to emphasize the importance of thought choice: What do you see?

opportunitiesnowhere

Do you perceive the message as "opportunities nowhere" or "opportunities now here"? To draw a parallel, do you see change as something to be feared or an opportunity to be seized? Like Abraham Lincoln, Walt Disney and Michael Jordan, a leader is one who makes the thought choice to be a "pursuer of the possible," rather than a "predictor of the inevitable."[32] The pessimist sees the difficulty in every opportunity, whereas the optimist sees the opportunity in every difficulty.

Our thoughts are so powerful that they can actually have an impact on our happiness, meaning that we can largely blame ourselves if we are not happy with our circumstances. As author and lexicographer Samuel Johnson wrote, "He who has so little knowledge of human nature as to seek happiness by changing anything but his own dispositions will waste his life in fruitless efforts and multiply the grief which he purposes to remove."

As is the case with happiness, most things in life flow from the inside outward. So, you can tell what's going on inside of a leader by what's going on around him or her. Your outer world of relationships often corresponds to your true inner personality; your outer world of health often corresponds to your inner attitudes of mind; your outer world of income and financial achievement often correspond to your inner world of thought and preparation. The conditions that you keep your home or car in will generally correspond to your state of mind at any particular time. When you are

> The only permanent way to change the outer things is to change the inner things.

feeling positive, confident and in control of your life, your home, your car, your workplace and even your closets will reflect order and effective management. The only permanent way to change the outer things is to change the inner things. William James, medical doctor and professor of psychology and philosophy at Harvard University, has stated "The greatest revolution of our generation is the discovery that human beings, by changing the inner attitude of their minds, can change the outer aspects of their lives."

Recognize and Manage Your Thoughts

If you wish to check on your true mental and spiritual condition, simply note your voluntary thoughts over the past few hours or days. What have you chosen to think about when free to think of whatever you pleased? Toward what has your inner heart turned when it was free to turn where it would? Such a test is easy to run. If we are honest with ourselves, we can discover not only what we are but also what we are going to become—we could soon be the sum of our voluntary thoughts.

Ponder the following and check whether you have thought or talked like this recently:

- I can't remember names.
- I just know it won't work.
- My stupid knee lets me down.
- I can't seem to get organized.
- I can't seem to lose weight.
- I am too shy.
- I just can't quit smoking.

- I'm really out of shape.
- I never win anything.
- I'll never get it right.
- If only I had more time.

Our internal programming mechanism treats everything we tell it with equal indifference. For example, when we say something like, "No matter what I do, I just can't seem to make ends meet," our subconscious says, "Okay, I'll do what you are telling me to do. I'll make sure you can't make ends meet." If our self-talk revolves only around our failures and defeats, guess what our future will be? I am a firm believer that your thoughts (and the way your mind operates) control your feelings, which create your attitudes, which create your actions, which create your results.

We cannot control our feelings, but we can control our thoughts. Our thoughts stir our feelings and, thus, strongly influence our will. Most of us can determine what we will think about. Of course, the troubled person may find his or her thoughts difficult to control, even while concentrating upon a worthy subject. There is nothing wrong with allowing yourself to feel and express your negative thoughts and emotions. Everyone has these. The key is not to let them run your life. To some extent, negative thoughts may help point us in a better direction or help us fulfill an unmet need (for example, the need to restore a

> We cannot control our feelings, but we can control our thoughts.

relationship or take care of physical health). The key is not to let negative thoughts run your life and to be aware that it is your choice to engage in these emotions.

The *New York Times* bestseller *My Stroke of Insight* tells the miraculous story of Jill Bolte Taylor, who was later named one of *Time* magazine's 100 Most Influential People in the World. In 1996, Taylor had a massive and debilitating stroke in the left hemisphere of her brain. As a Harvard brain scientist, she was able to study her own brain function and mental deterioration from the inside out. When the rational and logical left side of Jill's brain deteriorated, she was not able to walk or talk and completely lost her memory. Despite this, Jill experienced a wonderful, peaceful and euphoria-like state of mind, which she attributes to the intuitive, imaginative and carefree attributes of the right brain. The stroke was a life-changing revelation for Jill. It taught her that "'stepping to the right' of our left brains, we can uncover feelings of well-being and peace that are often sidelined by 'brain chatter.'"

Thankfully, after eight years, Jill completely recovered and now shares with others how they can control negative left-hemisphere thoughts. She teaches that we can experience an emotion for only 90 seconds. If the emotion continues, Taylor concludes, it is because we have allowed the thoughts created in our left brain to stay engaged in this emotion.

Taylor defines responsibility as

the ability to choose how we respond to stimulation coming in through our sensory systems at any moment in time. Although there are certain limbic system (emotional) programs that can be triggered automatically, it takes less than 90 seconds for one of these programs to be triggered, surge through our body, and then be completely flushed out of our bloodstream. My anger response, for example, is a programmed response that can be set off automatically. Once triggered, the chemical released by my brain surges through my body and I have a physiological experience. Within 90 seconds from the initial trigger, the chemical component of my anger has completely dissipated from my blood and my automatic response is over. If, however, I remain angry after those 90 seconds have passed, then it is because I have *chosen* to let that circuit continue to run.[33]

Changing your thoughts is not easy. In fact, it may be the hardest thing you ever do—but also the *most valuable*. Once you have made the decision to do something this important and valuable toward achieving your own ideal personal greatness, you absolutely must go on to changing your own mentality and thought choice. Your leadership effectiveness is determined by your mind's programming.

CHANGING YOUR THOUGHT CHOICE
Stay focused.
Think desires versus fears.
Expect success.
Talk to yourself.

Stay Focused

Recognize the danger of "playing" with thoughts that run contrary to your treasured convictions and vision. For example, I believe marriage is a monogamous and lifetime commitment. If I "play" with thinking such as "I don't know if this marriage is going to work. Just in case it doesn't, I better keep Ms. X in mind as my subsequent partner," then I have taken something away from my commitment to my wife, Mary Lynn. The more I think about Plan B, the more likely I am to need it!

Think Desires versus Fears

Two of the main categories of emotion are *desire* and *fear*. Most of our decisions are made on the basis of fear rather than desire. However, the more we make decisions because of fear, the more likely those circumstances are to be repeated. Most people are immobilized by their fears—the fear of poverty or loss, the fear of criticism or disapproval, the fear of ill health, the fear of being taken advantage of and so on. Above all, they fear failure and rejection to the point that they are willing to lead lives of quiet desperation rather than risk having any of their fears realized. The majority of the world's population live this way for most of their lives. The paradox is that the more you desire or fear something, the more likely you will attract it into your life.

So how do you stop fearing? The key is *to think only about what you desire*. Fear, after all, is simply false expectations appearing real. I keep my mind off what I fear and dwell on the things I want more of in life. Through my Mount Ruapehu experience, I learned that the mind is so powerful that

I must control it with great firmness, so that it is continually moving me in the direction I want to go. I eliminated my fear-filled thoughts on the mountain by substituting positive ones in their place. Choosing to think (and believe) positively had a calming effect upon me, especially as I faced the ice wall and the prospect of trying to survive a night at thirty degrees below zero. To stop thinking about the problem and to start thinking about the solution was how the seemingly impossible became possible.

Expect Success

Successful leaders have an attitude of confident, positive self-expectancy. They *expect* to be successful. They *expect* to be respected. They *expect* to be happy. Successful people don't have the negative expectations—for example, of cynicism and pessimism—that somehow cause situations to work out as expected. A perfect example is described by Robert Rosenthal in his book *Pygmalion in the Classroom.* His research concluded that the expectations of teachers had an enormous impact on the performance of students. He found that if students felt they were expected to do well, they did much better than they would have in the absence of those expectations. Think back to the expectations your parents or guardians set for you. Think about the expectations you set for your own children or loved ones. We're all unconsciously programmed to attempt to live up to, or down

> We're all unconsciously programmed to attempt to live up to, or down to, the expectations others had of us while we were growing up.

to, the expectations others had of us while we were growing up. And this instinctive need for approval usually outlives our parents. If those who raised you expected you to do well, and confidently and positively encouraged you to do your best and be your best, you have likely become the type of person who sets his or her sights high. However, many parents express their expectations in an unrealistic or negative way, which can put an unhealthy burden on children, making them feel that they can never measure up. Alternatively, some parents don't communicate expectations at all, potentially leaving their children even worse off.

The wonderful thing about expectations is that you can manufacture your own. You can create your own way of approaching the world, expecting the very best of yourself in every situation. Your expectations of yourself are in themselves powerful enough to override negative expectations that anyone else may have of you. You can create a forceful field of positive mental energy around you by confidently expecting to gain something from every situation. Since they are completely under your control, make sure that your expectations are consistent with what you want to happen. The power of positive expectations alone can change your whole personality, your leadership and enable your influence to grow.

Author W. Clement Stone is famous for being an "inverse paranoid." An inverse paranoid is a person who believes that the universe is conspiring to do him or her *good*. Inverse paranoids see every situation as one that is heaven-sent either to confer some benefit or teach some valuable lesson to help them be even more successful. This state of being is the foundation of a positive mental attitude.

I have two suggestions for starting your day with expectations of success and thereby initiating the probability that success will come. Each morning when you open the curtains, say, "Good morning, God!" rather than "Good God—morning." *Expect the best and enjoy it.* Do this enough times to make it a habit. Also, if you say out loud, "I believe something wonderful is going to happen to me today," you'll find that it's more likely to be the case. The opposite is certainly true, too.

Talk to Yourself

Continually correct and shift negative attitudes into positive, action-oriented ones by using self-talk. Correction involves a shift in the mind and a mental commitment to change. Self-talk is the means by which thought choice and correction operate. We direct our subconscious minds to stop doing something in one way and start doing it in another.

Self-talk is "speaking" and listening to our thought choices internally as a way of monitoring our thoughts. Between our ears, we have a microcosm of what happens between people as they relate to one another. How we treat ourselves is a key determinant of how we treat others; how we lead ourselves determines how we lead others. Because our talk to others is drawn from the same cognitive "bank" as that in which we deposit our own self-talk, unless we learn to do differently, we pass on our own programming to our followers and our children. Statements such as "You never listen to me" or "You'll never amount to anything" are far from harmless, especially for the young, impressionable minds of children.

Have you ever been to a pep rally and found the "pep" lasted only until the next day? Have you ever read a self-help book or listened to a CD, felt inspired to change, begun to change and then simply "fizzled out"? Where did the inspiration disappear to? The problem is not with the books, tapes, CDs or talks. A lot of self-help ideas *should* work and *could* work. Our amazing brain, the incredibly powerful personal computer between our ears, is capable of doing anything reasonable that we would like it to do—*but we have to know how to use it*. If we talk to it appropriately, it will do the appropriate thing. As with a computer, if we give our mind the wrong directions, it will act on those wrong directions. It will continue to respond to the negative programming that we and the rest of the world have been giving it. Unfortunately, negative programming is the dominant form of self-talk (we tend to be our own severest critic), and it originates from parents, teachers, associates, the media and people's general tendency to complain, criticize and put down. In fact, psychologists estimate that 70 per cent of our thoughts are negative.[34] And since we become the living result of our thoughts, how successfully we lead is inexorably tied to the words and beliefs that we store in our mind.

One of the "rules" of the brain is to accept ideas that are similar to existing beliefs. The more you think about anything in a particular way, the more you will believe that *that* is how it really is. The longer you have bought the thought, the truer it is. Therefore, negative self-talk does nothing other than solidify self-made walls of self-defeat. Your subconscious

> How successfully we lead is inexorably tied to the words and beliefs that we store in our mind.

mind works day and night to make sure you will become precisely what you have described yourself to be. Be aware that much of our self-talk will remain unnoticed by our conscious minds—it may be silent or consist only of quiet nudges, self-doubt, unspoken fears of failure or a nagging discomfort that things just aren't right.

When you decide to stop thinking negatively, if you do not have a positive vocabulary to take the place of the negative one, you will invariably return to the negative self-talk of the past. Self-talk uses the conscious mind for reprogramming (as an aside, hypnosis uses the unconscious mind). That is, the self-talk technique incorporates the principle of personal responsibility. Whether self-talk is silent, spoken aloud, written or tape-recorded, it must be specific and delivered in the present tense—that is, stated as if the desired change is simply a fact.

Please do one thing for yourself. You may feel silly doing it, but trust me—it is powerful! Write a short list of three to five things you want to believe about yourself. Say these statements out loud to yourself as many times as you can each day. Here are some examples of positive self-talk scripts, which, when repeated, will reprogram your mind:

- I control the thoughts I choose. No thought, at any time, can dwell in my mind without my approval or permission.
- When I meet a new problem, I do not see the problem as my enemy. I know that finding the solution to the problem will move me forward in my own personal growth.

- I am in control of my feelings, my emotions, my attitudes and my needs. I control them; they do not control me.
- I can do anything I believe I can do! I have talents, skills and abilities.
- Today is a *great* day. I've got what it takes, so I choose to do it right, do it well. I choose to live today with joy and with love. I rejoice and am glad for the gift of today.
- Not everyone will like or respect the decisions that are best for me and my family. That is okay, and it does not diminish my self-worth.
- I strive for work–life balance. I can set priorities based on what is important to me. I can control what time I leave the office. I can comfortably ask for help when I need it.
- I enjoy the work I do and find purpose in it.

The Mount Ruapehu experience taught me the overwhelmingly important truth that I will become what I spend my time thinking of. The brain simply believes what you tell it most often, and it will create that reality. With our minds, we control most things in our lives, including our health, relationships, careers and leadership abilities. Since the night on Ruapehu, I have had countless hours to reflect, recall, dream (although they're sometimes nightmares) and analyze that experience minute by minute. What I prayed, what I focused upon—specifically, how I talked to myself and what I said—I now understand, provided the fundamental key to my survival and the ability to accomplish what seemed impossible.

My own self-talk that day and night was simply *a dialogue with God*. It included prayer, often literally yelling to (and at) God and listening to his voice inside me, and talking to myself, often out loud in spite of being alone. To claim that I self-talked my way out of crisis and away from the clutches of death would be an exaggeration. But as I look back at the details of that night, I see that what I said was profoundly significant. Whether it was said aloud or silently, to God or to myself, I intuitively did not believe it to be irrelevant, although the particulars are blurry in my memory. And that's okay with me because what I recall most vividly is the peace and internal calm that flooded through my near frozen body when I read and dwelt on the words that jumped out from the Gideon Bible: "I can do all things through Christ, who strengthens me." This idea reverberated inside my head for the duration of the night. It became the script for and source of much of my self-talk. I remember repeating the line out loud, emphasizing a different word each time I spoke it. (Language studies suggest that 38 per cent of meaning is translated via intonation.[35]) To the people who are tempted to dismiss this part of my story as "brainwashing," I confidently reply and challenge, "So? What's your point?" I took responsibility for choosing my thoughts and focus. I intentionally controlled my mind's activity as much as I could by deliberately repeating countless times that affirming and energizing line. I learned that I *do* have control over what I say to myself and how I say it and that, therefore, I must take responsibility for the content and tone of my self-talk.

Another example of my self-talk on Mount Ruapehu was repeatedly counting, "one, two, three, four, five," before I released the air from my lungs. I also thanked God for getting me through each five-second period. I told myself—and I believed—that I would make it through the next five-second breathing phase. The principle underlying this repetition was that of breaking the time down into manageable bites. I got through the longest night of my life five seconds at a time.

I am convinced that it was because of the underpinnings of this particular "programming vocabulary" that my self-talk got me through the night.

The self-talk involved my *programming* . . . that I am an "overcomer." I kept repeating this to myself. I grew up in New Zealand, which is a do-it-yourself culture. During the world wars, the Kiwis gained the reputation of being gifted at creatively using whatever was available to overcome any problem they faced. Perhaps growing up in an environment that lacked the toys and material abundance that most North American children today take for granted formed the roots of my programming as a survivor. Necessity does become the mother of invention when a youngster doesn't have many supplies but has the desire and vision to make a scooter—he designs and creates a steering system using hinge flanges and four-inch nails.

The self-talk involved my *beliefs* . . . that God loves me and will take care of me. Leaders with different beliefs must maintain their own faith-centred leadership based on those beliefs, whatever they may be. Remember that belief does not require something to be true. It requires only that we believe that it is true. This is profound! It means that our own reality is based upon what each of us believes—whether it is true or not.

The self-talk involved my *attitude* . . . of hope. This is the predominate perspective from which I view life. I believe that it is my identity as a child of God that allowed me before Ruapehu, after Ruapehu and certainly during Ruapehu to maintain an attitude of hope and positive anticipation. My self-talk included reminders that God is in control, which made me feel safe and assured that ultimately, one way or another, I would be okay. A positive attitude may spring from a source other than God's role in one's life; for example, your attitude may be drawn from the love of your family or a significant event in your past that continually reminds you of your good fortune.

The self-talk involved my *feelings* . . . of tranquility. While I initially felt despair, my feelings changed dramatically when I turned to page 1,048 of the Gideon Bible. Although I was physically numb because of the extreme cold, a series of waves of tranquility burst from the very centre of my pain and grief. In hindsight, I am convinced it was no accident that I experienced these waves of peace and a readiness to die. At the time, I had been including in my seminars the teaching and personal conviction that there is always a gift in the middle of hardship and sorrow—if you look for it. At least a year before facing death on the mountaintop, I had coined the saying, "The valley is where the fertile soil is." People often associate pits or valleys with the lows or depression points in life. However, the most fertile soil is usually washed to the valley. We all experience "valleys" in our lives. Rejoice!

Talk to yourself instead of allowing your self to talk to you. "Most of your unhappiness in life is due to the fact that you are listening to yourself instead of talking to yourself."[36] You have a responsibility to think about what is uplifting, pure, right, healthy, encouraging and, most of all, true. Speak to yourself about these sorts of things instead of allowing your condemning and worrying self to speak to you.

To accomplish the seemingly impossible, leaders have to look inside themselves and take responsibility for their success—or lack of success. As you have surely heard before, you get back what you put in—no more, no less. *And you can determine and take control of what you put in.* No one will ever take a breath for us. No one will ever think a thought that is ours. No one will ever experience what happens to us, dream our dreams or cry our tears. The "self" and the divine spirit that drives it are what we have and what we are. No one can ever live a moment of our lives for us. That we must do for ourselves. That is our responsibility. Perhaps the most important personal choice a leader can make is to accept responsibility for everything he or she will be. Taking personal responsibility is what separates the superior leader from the average leader. Accepting responsibility is also the foundation of high self-esteem, personal pride and self-respect.

While thoughts are deeply powerful, it is action that ignites meeting our goals. However, action involves first stepping out and taking that leap of faith. Believing in and trusting our thoughts stimulates action. We will take that step of faith together in the next chapter.

TAKE FIVE SECONDS

Point to Ponder
We can't control our feelings, but we can control our thoughts about them.

Quotes to Remember
"It's choice—not chance—that determines your destiny." —*Jean Nidetch*

"You are not only responsible for what you say, but also for what you do not say." —*Martin Luther*

"The primary cause of unhappiness is never the situation but your thoughts about it." —*Eckhart Tolle*

"Be transformed by the renewing of your mind."
—*Romans 12:2*

"A man is what he thinks about all day long."
—*Ralph Waldo Emerson*

"I don't think of all the misery, but of all the beauty that still remains. . . . Whoever is happy will make others happy, too." —*Anne Frank*

Question to Consider
What self-talk can I practise today?

6

GET INTO THE WHEELBARROW
FAITH AND ACTION

"Faith is taking the first step even when you
don't see the whole staircase."
—*Martin Luther King Jr.*

I will never forget the words that teaching inspector Joshua Weinstein wrote across the top of my workbook during the first year of my teaching career: "Walk the path in which you have faith." He was Jewish, and I am a Christian. He avoided preaching at me but instead pointed to the need for me to teach, walk and live in congruence with whatever belief system I had. I believed then, as I do today, that the Lord was looking after me throughout that year and my subsequent years of teaching and that he was also present at the peak of Mount Ruapehu, just as he is at the desk at which I am currently sitting.

I believe that my being a man of faith (that is, one who not only believes in God's existence, power, presence, mercy and grace but whose belief system is the cornerstone of his existence) is the prime reason my prayers were answered that cold night in May. I distinctly remember the despairing realization that the hut I was climbing toward was farther away than I had thought it would be. Already exhausted to the point of not being able to lift myself any further, I saw the ice wall that loomed up between the hut and me. I looked to the sky, prayed for safety and heard the words, "I can do all things through Christ who strengthens me."

It is possible that these words were spoken by my inner voice and not audible words spoken from outside my body. However, not only mountaineers but also divers, prisoners of war, sailors, astronauts, explorers and 9/11 survivors—people who survived against all odds—have reported similar experiences time and time again. John Geiger, historian, bestselling author and governor of the Royal Canadian Geographical Society, scientifically analyzed the survival stories of numerous people who had attained guidance and help from an outside source, or what he calls "the Third Man." In his book *The Third Man Factor*, John asks, "If the Third Man is caused by 'decay of brain functions' [as has been argued] . . . why then would it offer such support, so different from conventional hallucinations with their attendant sense of unreality?" John concludes, "Appearances of the Third Man are in no way characteristic of delirium. . . . It begins with a belief, a belief that a companion stands with them." John stresses the words of climber Greg Child, "Those who have experienced the other presence make a distinction between it and hallucinations, which often misguide and disorient. The presence seems much more real, assisting by either guiding or allaying fears with companionship.'"[37]

I choose to interpret my momentous experience as I ascended that mountain as God speaking to me, and I believe that had Bruce or anyone else been beside me, he too would have heard the same words. However, if you, the reader, choose to believe that the words came from within me, they certainly prove the existence and significance of our inner voice as discussed in Chapter 4. My inner voice is rooted in a spirit of faith, and the words of encouragement I heard reminded me where my real strength lay. The ten-foot vertical wall of ice that threatened to stand between me and the presumed safety of the hut was surmounted because God was there propelling my continued action, eventually enabling me to clutch the wooden supports of the hut.

What is faith, and how can it be applied by a leader regardless of his or her belief system? Faith can be described as "the substance of things hoped for, the evidence of things unseen" (Hebrews 11:1, NIV). As poet Patrick Overton explains it in his poem "Faith,"

> When you walk to the edge of all the light you have
> and take that first step into the darkness of the unknown,
> you must believe that one of two things will happen:
>
> There will be something solid for you to stand upon,
> or, you will be taught how to fly.

How does faith fuel action? Although they can see only so far, leaders must be willing to go as far as they can see with the confidence that when they get there, the path ahead will be lit. They must make decisions and act, often without having 100 per cent of the information needed. Michael McCain, CEO of Maple Leaf Foods, describes the times when decisions have to be made as "moments of truth." A leader has to make a choice, have faith in that choice and move the organization forward to support and execute that choice.

Heroic leaders tend to be normal people who have extraordinary demands placed on them and who triumphantly rise to the occasion. For example, Mother Teresa considered herself "a pencil in the hand of God." She also added, "He has not called me to be successful but to be faithful."

> Leaders must be willing to go as far as they can see with the confidence that when they get there, the path ahead will be lit.

Although I believe God gives us free will, I also believe he guides us when we "listen" to him. If I am of a certain opinion, I will not change that opinion unless I gain clear leadership from God to do so, so I ask for guidance. Once I feel assured that I am making the right decision, I have the confidence to act. I can then pass on this confidence effectively to the team that I am leading.

My survival on the mountain, as well as my own business success, involved two principles, which are separate yet interdependent aspects of faith: *belief* and *trust*.

Belief

What you can see in your mind and *believe* in your heart, you will achieve. A leader must conceive the vision, but without genuinely believing in it, he or she will, predictably, not be able to accomplish, nor motivate a team to accomplish, the goal. As Henry Ford stated, "Whether you think that you can or think that you can't, you are usually right."

I believed I could reach the hut, even when the ice wall was blocking my way. I had had a profound spiritual experience when God's words enabled me to believe I could "do all things." In addition, my faith in God's promise made it so much easier to believe that I would overcome the obstacles before me. As a leader, you need to evaluate or strengthen your own belief system. As Joshua Weinstein said to me, "Walk the path in which *you* have faith."

The Power in What You Believe

Whatever you believe with conviction and feeling becomes your reality. The more intensely you believe something to be true, the more likely it *will* be true for you. To really believe something, you cannot imagine it to be otherwise. For example, your beliefs would edit out or cause you to ignore incoming information that is inconsistent with what you have decided to believe, such as people telling you, "It isn't possible."

American psychologist, philosopher, doctor and author William James said, "Belief creates the actual fact." Scripture states, "As you believed, so will it happen to you" (Matthew 9:29, WENT). You may not necessarily believe what you see, but you *see* what you believe. For example, if you absolutely believe you were meant to be a great success, then no matter what happens, you will press forward toward your leadership goals. On the other hand, if you believe success is a matter of luck, accident or being in the right place at the right time, then you may be easily discouraged or disappointed when things do not work out as you'd planned. Your beliefs set you up for either success or failure.

We generally look at the world either from a benevolent point of view or a malevolent point of view. If you have a benevolent world view, you generally believe the world is a decent place to live in. You tend to see the good in people and situations and to believe there is plenty of opportunity around you, of which you can take advantage. You are primarily optimistic. People with a malevolent world view harbour a generally negative or pessimistic attitude toward themselves and others. The malevolent person sees injustice, oppression and misfortune everywhere. When things go wrong, they usually blame it on bad luck or bad people and feel victimized. Needless to say, optimistic people tend to be the movers and the shakers, the builders and the creators and, of course, the leaders. Upbeat and cheerful, they by and large respond positively and constructively to the inevitable ups and downs of everyday life.

Ideally, your outer behaviour is consistent with your inner beliefs. This is sometimes referred to as "inside-out leadership." Even if our walk is not always in sync with our talk, we can accurately predict that our walk will be consistent with our dominant beliefs about ourselves and others.

Perhaps the biggest mental blocks that we have to overcome are those contained in our *self-limiting beliefs*. These are the beliefs that hold us back and often cause us to see things in a way that simply is not real. Most of our self-limiting beliefs are based on negative information we have taken in and accepted as true despite their not being true at all. The good news is that you can train your mind to think in a habitually positive way, dispelling such myths. Choosing your thoughts wisely, as discussed in Chapter 5, can help you shape your beliefs.

Positive Thinking Must Include Positive Believing

Positive believing goes well beyond the positive thinking concepts discussed in the previous chapter. Whereas attempting to push the mind beyond its limitations will only result in moving from the world of reality to one of fantasy, faith transcends the limitations of the mind and incorporates the real but unseen world. The believer's faith is as valid as its object. Beliefs are like unquestioned commands, telling us how things are, what is possible, what is not possible and what can and cannot be done. Beliefs shape every thought, every feeling and every action we experience. Spanish poet Antonio Machado said, "Under all that we think lives all that we believe, like the ultimate veil of our spirit."

If you raise your standards but don't really believe you can meet them, you have sabotaged yourself. For example, research has proven that medical procedures have a much greater chance of success if the patient fully believes in them.[38] Patients' beliefs in the possibility of recovery and in the competence of medical practitioners play a large role in the healing process. Cancer patients who live the longest are unusual individuals who do not become anxious or depressed; rather, they are reported to have faith and inner confidence.[39] Success relies on the patient's willingness to participate in his or her own mental and physical well-being.

Trust

Henry L. Stimson said, "The only way to make a man trustworthy is to trust him; and the surest way to make him untrustworthy is to distrust him and show your distrust."

While leaders must believe in themselves, their team and their vision, truly effective leaders must go a step further and actually move beyond believing to *trusting*. The following story illustrates the key difference between these two elements of faith and why trust is recognized as the *ultimate intangible* for a successful leader.

The senior management team of Windsor Wheelbarrow Ltd.'s annual weekend retreat at the Hilton Hotel overlooking Niagara Falls had proven very fruitful.

President and CEO Bill Fluter, who had led most of the strategic planning sessions, had spared no expense for the accommodations, meals and hospitality room. He'd even sat down at the piano Saturday evening and led a good old-fashioned singalong after dinner.

Satisfied with the work accomplished, everyone was in a good mood when Bill announced he had arranged a surprise and requested that the whole team meet the following morning after breakfast at a designated spot by the railing on the Canadian side of the falls. He didn't give details but just said, "Be there at ten." Everyone assumed Bill had a reason to close the retreat in this fashion and figured this might be his way of thanking the team for another good year and a successful planning session.

Bill was absent from breakfast the next morning, but the team dutifully assembled by the falls at ten. The roar of the water, the mist it created and the cool, overcast weather made everybody huddle together, pulling their raincoats and jackets around themselves to keep as dry as possible. The team began to ask one another, "What's this all about?" Yes, the majesty of the falls was inspiring, and yes, it was little surprise that this was one of the wonders of the world, but "Where's Bill, and what's he up to?"

Peter was the first to notice the large steel spike that had been driven into the ground a few feet away from where the team stood. Once he pointed it out, they all wondered about the function of the steel cable that extended from the spike and disappeared into the huge cloud of spray billowing up from the cascading waters.

Gayle let out a scream as she pointed to a sight that froze the whole group. Everyone stared with astonishment at the figure walking toward them through the mist. Was it a ghost? Were they hallucinating?

Coming toward them, balancing on the steel cable, was a man dressed in a bright yellow raincoat. If that wasn't enough of a stunt, he was pushing a wheelbarrow in front of him!

The obvious danger, the certainty of instant death if he slipped, made the group gasp with wonder and fright. The man methodically put one foot in front of the other, pushing the wheelbarrow closer and closer to the bank.

Raj blurted out, "It's . . . it's Bill!"

Peter yelled, "Good grief . . . it's our wheelbarrow!"

Fear gripped the entire team as the reality of what they were goggling at sank into their minds.

"But . . . hey, Bill . . . be careful, be careful!" screamed Renee. It was then that something happened that, while unplanned, seemed unconditionally appropriate. Spontaneously, each grabbed someone else's hand and ran as a single line to the spot where the spike anchored the cable.

"Look at that," Maria said, and the others knew what was astonishing her. Time seemed to slow down, allowing everyone to marvel at Bill's ingenuity and extreme courage.

"Is he crazy?" changed to words of amazement as the onlookers could now see how Bill was doing the seemingly impossible. He had taken the rubber tire off the wheel, so that the concave rim fit snugly on the steel cable, giving a stable point of contact. Bill firmly grasped each of the handles on the wheelbarrow, creating a three-point shape of stability, which enabled him to stand upright and move slowly toward his team.

As Raj recognized the triangle as the most stable geometric shape, Sarah whispered, "Oh my God, oh my God . . . ," and Tom, who had a reputation of being the cheerleader of the team, screamed out over the roar of the falls, "Bill, keep coming! We're here to get you. You can do it! You're ama-a-a-zing!"

The others joined in, and when Bill pushed the wheelbarrow beyond the bank, everybody was either screaming encouragement or simply crying.

The team extended their arms toward their leader, and once he had bounced the wheelbarrow to the ground and stood on terra firma himself, they simply clutched him, gasping, crying and expressing joy, mingled with enormous relief. The entire senior team huddled together for a good ten seconds before their grips loosened and a most memorable debriefing session began.

Bill stood tall and calmly dismissed the expressions of "Why?" "Have you lost it?" "You're crazy!" "Amazing feat!" "What were you thinking?" and held up his hand until the group fell silent. With an actor's skill, he paused and looked from the eyes of one team member to those of the next. When he had their rapt attention, he asked, "Do you believe what you have seen here this morning?"

The "not really's" changed to an agreed-upon recognition of Bill's near-miraculous accomplishment, and someone finally said, "Yes, we believe you did it."

"Okay," said Bill. "Here's the key question: Do you believe I could do it again?"

A pause of intense thought was interrupted by expressions of "I'm not certain," "Maybe," "Sure," "Of course you could" and "Why try?"

Again Bill held up his hand and pointedly asked, "Did you with your own eyes see me walk along the rope?"

"Yes."

"Okay, I will ask you again. Do you have faith in me? Do you believe I can do it again?"

Eventually, the entire team agreed, "Yes," and a wave of cohesion bonded the individuals into an all-powerful whole. Unanimously, they cheered, "Yes, we do have faith in you; we do believe you can do it again."

Bill took a deep breath, again took time to eyeball every team member, grasped the handles of the wheelbarrow, bounced it onto the rope and in a calm and gentle yet assertive voice said "Okay, get into the wheelbarrow!"

This dramatically demonstrates the difference between belief and trust. It is good to believe and have faith in someone or something, but it is trust that moves mountains.

When I was on Mount Ruapehu, I had to trust my abilities and my faith. I had to take action, and I chose to climb upward despite my anguish over the whereabouts of my brother-in-law. I believed in myself and envisioned my survival. Each succeeding foot grip was a step out in faith. To survive, I had to keep stepping forward. Just one deliberate step at a time and then a breath of praise. Letting my grief get the best of me or staying in the same place would have resulted in my death. I had to let my fear go and give the night up to a higher power.

Trust requires both action (for example, stepping into the wheelbarrow rather than only offering claims of faith) and letting go. When Bruce pulled back his hand to avoid seizing mine and pulling me with him down the mountain, he "let go"—completely gave up control—in order to save my life. Tears well up in my eyes at this memory, as what he did is the most selfless thing anyone has ever done for me. Bruce let go so that I wouldn't be dragged down with him. This action of love is a genuine reflection of how he cared for the people in his life. For me, this book is a way of both letting go and sharing what I have learned with the hope of helping others. Take a minute to ponder these questions: Do you genuinely care for people? What actions or inactions are holding you back? What do you need to let go of? What do you need to trust more?

Trust is the ultimate intangible. It has no shape or substance, yet it empowers our actions. Its presence or absence governs our behaviour as if it were a real, physical force. Trust is the principle that most clearly assists us in discriminating between real leaders and false prophets. Credibility, influence, ability to gain buy-in from followers, personal power and the talent to elicit greatness from others all boil down primarily to trustworthiness and having trust in others. It is universally acknowledged that trust can lead to repeat business, the extension of credit and reduced employee turnover. Business people do not simply have an inherent virtue that makes them stick to their word or pay their bills promptly. They must realize that their bread is buttered by the faith others have in their reliability. Think of trust as an asset, like money in your pocket or in an organization's treasury. We can grasp the real utility of this resource if we view trust as a miracle currency. It can be either accumulated and spent—without necessarily depleting our reserves—or lost, so that we become destitute.

> Trust requires both action and letting go.

The belief that we live in a reasonably predictable world is the basis on which trust is built and the basis of our plans and actions. Would you cross a bridge, post a parcel, confide in a friend or work at a job without trust that the bridge will hold, the parcel will be delivered, the friend will keep the confidence or you will be paid for your labour? Living without such measures of trust would confine us to perpetual fears, paranoia, inefficiency and inaction. Trust is the "miracle ingredient" in an organizational life—a lubricant that reduces friction and a catalyst that facilitates action. Based on repetitive transactions yielding consistent results, trust begins our initial period of extending. In new situations, we "extend" a degree of trust. As our efforts provoke responses, we take appropriate action, withholding or extending our involvement. While we need to be alert for danger signals, we also need to extend enough trust to go forward.

Trust is not simply "blind faith," nor is it lemming-like followership. It is a belief and hope that trustworthiness will continue. Trust can be represented by the level and relative stability (or precariousness) of what author Stephen Covey calls the "emotional bank account balance." When a leader makes enough positive emotional deposits in a relationship with a follower, the follower will trust the leader. For this reason, trust is highly influenced by what has happened most recently. If the expectation of a result tends to produce that result, then trust can pay off. However, *genuine* belief is necessary. If you try to produce results through trust without really *believing* that people are trustworthy, you will set up a different self-fulfilling prophecy. By expecting failure, you will get it!

An organization's ineffectiveness largely reflects distrust. If employees compete viciously and pull colleagues down rather than co-operating, everyone pays a price. If overcritical managers berate employees, the employees are foolish to extend their trust. If managers play "good guys/bad guys" with other departments, they diminish trust between groups and promote interdepartmental bickering. If executives behave in irresponsible ways that are later revealed in the press, both public trust and organizational trust are destroyed.

Trust is the residue of promises fulfilled. To gain it requires truth-telling and promise-keeping. Truth, by eliminating lies and falsehoods, clears the way for trust. Broken promises, on the other hand, chip away at it. Trust ultimately peaks when we respect others by listening seriously to their ideas or opinions. When an organization communicates its values and rewards employees for living up to them, it builds a foundation that allows trust to grow. Leaders create trust by being consistent, predictable and dependable.

Trust and Delegation

Trust is the foundation of delegation, which by definition means giving up control (that is, letting go) and yet maintaining responsibility. One of the reasons some companies' growth is stalled is that their leaders have poor delegation skills. "As a business grows, the limited amount of time a manager has will quickly be absorbed by executing various tasks until there is no time left to take on anything new. Effective, growth-oriented companies have management teams that excel in delegation as they grow."[40]

In *Thriving on Chaos,* Tom Peters quotes an American Management Association (AMA) brief, which reported that 37 per cent of a manager's time is spent checking up on others, covering behinds, justifying past decisions, defending past actions or taking on similar unproductive activities.[41] Such tasks are too often regarded as necessary, but seldom are their costs calculated so that their time consequences can be evaluated. It is hard to get much work done when you are constantly looking over your shoulder and engaging in "rear-end-covering" activities.

I have realized the importance of empowering employees to do the job they were hired to do and to be the best workers they can be. This requires believing in them, having (and communicating) strong expectations and trusting them to get the job done. The goal is for employees to be able to say, "We did it ourselves."

Knowing the right questions to ask is a key step in delegating and empowering others. Leaders should know the right questions to ask but shouldn't necessarily know all the answers. After all, if you give people every solution, eventually every problem will turn up at your desk. Asking "who?"—not "how?"—is another way to become better at delegating. People with perfectionist tendencies often have a hard time delegating and giving up control. However, success requires realizing that you have to learn to trust your subordinates and believe in their capabilities (which means that you don't feel the need to check up on them excessively). If you have employees you cannot trust, this probably means they are not the right fit for the job and you should consider providing them with serious coaching or even removing them from the organization.

Building Trusting Relationships

To build greater trust between you and your employees or followers, consider the following suggestions:[42]

- *Analyze the work.* Distribute challenging opportunities fairly, and set high but realistic expectations.
- *Train your followers* in how an assignment could be done, describe acceptable results and possible pitfalls, and then give them freedom to innovate in carrying out their tasks.
- *Focus on what gets done* rather than on how it gets done; avoid restrictive policies when possible and allow reasonable risk-taking.
- *Avoid using coercive power.* Progressively empower

your followers by delegating authority to them in every possible instance.

- When things go wrong or when mistakes are made, *concentrate on solving the problem*, rather than spending time and effort on punishment.
- *Skip the search for who is guilty,* and organize people to make sure things go right next time. Visualize and communicate what a correctly done job looks like.
- *Support your followers and help them to come out winners.* Followers trust leaders who offer them real opportunities, prepare them well, encourage them and enable them to demonstrate what they can do.

In *Learning to Lead*, Warren Bennis and Joan Goldsmith point out that trust provides the motivation and energy that make it possible for organizations to work at all. It is what motivates heroism, sells products and keeps communication humming. Trust is the source of organizational integrity. Leaders who garner trust generally exhibit the following qualities: vision, empathy, consistency and integrity.

In summary, faith-centred leadership is possible when you believe in yourself, in your vision and in your team, and trust your team enough to empower its members to make decisions. Without taking these initial steps of faith, your big rocks will always remain in the same place you left them. Accomplishing the seemingly impossible requires action; action involves taking calculated risks. And even then, the journey may require a few steps backward in order to move forward.

The principle of correction is essential to keeping yourself on track and is discussed in the next chapter.

Points to Ponder

Trust is a step beyond belief.

Belief and trust are two aspects of faith.

Faith inspires action and helps leaders accomplish the seemingly impossible.

Quotes to Remember

"I know that faith made my life possible and that of many others like me. . . . In my doubly shadowed world, faith gives me a reason for trying to draw harmony out of a marred instrument. Faith is not a cushion for me to fall back upon; it is my working energy." —*Helen Keller*

"Sure I am that this day, now, we are the masters of our fate. That the task which has been set us is not above our strength. That its pangs and toils are not beyond our endurance. As long as we have faith in our cause, and an unconquerable willpower, salvation will not be denied us." —*Winston Churchill*

Question to Consider

What fears do I need to let go of in my life so that I can better trust myself and those around me?

7

READY, FIRE, AIM
CORRECTION

*"A man who has committed a mistake and doesn't
correct it is committing another mistake."*
—*Confucius*

The absolute necessity for leaders to internalize and practise
the principle of correction in order to be successful cannot
be overemphasized. The Japanese term *kaizen*, meaning constant improvement, is pertinent to a discussion of correction
and can be illustrated through my Ruapehu mountaintop
experience. At the most critical point on the mountaintop, it
became immediately clear to me that I had to change both
my thoughts and my behaviour; however, actually correcting
my behaviour was extremely difficult.

The first mistake I'd made was letting Bruce take the full load of the pack. Initially, we had planned to take our own packs; however, being the generous and loving man he was, Bruce insisted on carrying my load of food and warm clothing, all of which plummeted down the mountain with him. The parallel to leadership is strong: Never let one team member carry the entire load because (a) a team working together is stronger than one member working alone and (b) if that member working alone falters, all is lost.

When I finally made it to the entrance of the hut to find food, shelter and help, I realized at once my second huge mistake. Cutting my way through the ice on the door would require enormous energy, which I couldn't afford to squander. But at that point, I had no choice. Once in the hut, my overwhelming tiredness culminated in my collapsing on the floor. My realization that I'd made a mistake was amplified once I saw the hut did not have a phone or any other mode of communication nor any survival supplies. My error in judgment and the danger in assuming some form of help would be there hit me like the proverbial ton of bricks.

It was now almost dark and the temperature was sinking rapidly. I was dressed only in a T-shirt and shorts and had no food or water. "Oh, Lord, please help! There's nothing here!" Almost at the same time as I uttered these words, a thought came to mind that probably originated from the wisdom of my father when I was still young: "It's not your falling down that matters; whether you pick yourself up is what really counts."

I was now at a most significant choice point. Do I deem

this so serious a problem as to justify giving up, or do I gather the courage and wisdom to use the crisis as a chance to regroup, redirect my efforts and ultimately correct my behaviour? While seemingly simple, and now relatively easy to talk about, the actual doing was (and remains) surprisingly difficult.

Let me illustrate by asking the following question:

> Question: There were six frogs on a log. Two of them decided to jump off. How many were left?
> Answer: Six.
> Reasoning: *Deciding* is not doing.

We've all heard the saying, "When the going gets tough, the tough get going." Yet, I don't believe it was simply "toughness" that prompted me to get up off the floor of the hut and see what I could find. I was physically exhausted, and rather than toughness, I attribute my regrouping and "correcting" to my having established a habit of recognizing that even in times of crises, there are opportunities to correct and learn, rather than reasons to quit or lower expectations. This is probably why Napoleon defined a leader as "a dealer in hope" and why Winston Churchill highlighted courage as a prerequisite to leadership.

In recent years, I have enjoyed asking the following question in a number of my seminars: "On July 20, 1969, Neil Armstrong was the first person to walk on the moon. What percentage of time did this history-making rocket stay precisely on track?" The answer contains a kernel of wisdom that has profound implications for leadership success. Participants in my seminars usually guess, calling out numbers such as 99.9 per cent, 50 per cent, 85 per cent. Rarely have I met anyone who is aware that, according to NASA, the rocket was exactly on track for a mere 3 per cent of the time it was in space.

For the vast majority of the journey, the rocket was "off track." Had it not been corrected by means of the sophisticated computers down on earth at the Houston base, it wouldn't have made history by landing. The humbling (yet encouraging) truth is that 97 per cent of the time, leaders who are destined to make enormous contributions to the world are missing the mark. Simply knowing this enables us to keep going even when things look very tough. Leaders who achieve the seemingly impossible are flexible and adaptable and seek constant feedback, whether it's from customers or team members, in order to make the changes necessary to keep them on target. Goal accomplishment is the art of correction, not protection.

> The humbling (yet encouraging) truth is that 97 per cent of the time, leaders who are destined to make enormous contributions to the world are missing the mark.

Some corporate philosophies have been reinvented to read, "ready, fire, aim," rather than the commonly expressed phrase "ready, aim, fire." The principle of correction is implied here, as successful leaders invariably demonstrate a bias toward action and a readiness to change. The successful leader tends not to be a perfectionist. A perfectionist is one who takes great pains—and passes them on to others! We must remember that we will make mistakes. A fundamental truth I affirmed on Mount Ruapehu is that you begin, you act, you correct. This guideline is especially important for leaders in positions of significant responsibility.

Admitting the Mistake and Holding Yourself Accountable

Before we can take steps toward change, we must openly and genuinely admit the mistake itself. Leaders who are self-aware and regularly take time to step back and reflect on their day and their actions are generally stronger in acknowledging and admitting their mistakes. I once knew an employee who performed extremely well. His metrics (plant efficiencies, yields, waste, etc.) were better than those of any other employee. However, he often cut corners to boost his metrics at the expense of other factors, such as listening to the concerns of his workers. Instead of owning up to these mistakes, he would sweep them under the carpet and hope no one would find out. When the mistakes were disclosed (from upset workers who felt they hadn't been treated fairly), I approached this person directly, and he again denied that he had done anything wrong. I asked him, "What makes you afraid of admitting you messed up?" He answered, "I fear that people will look down on me for making the mistake and respect me less." We had a fruitful conversation, and he now supports that owning up to a bad decision and making people aware of it—before it circulates back to him—is a professional behaviour. Doing so confirms self-awareness and assures managers that when you make a mistake (which happens to all of us!), you understand what happened, know how to correct it and also know what you will do differently next time. It is not the mistake that matters, but how you handle it. Good managers and friends will forgive and sometimes even embrace your mistakes—if you handle them with professional integrity.

Michael McCain, named 2008 CEO of the year by the Canadian Press, is an outstanding example of a leader who held himself accountable. Amid a listeriosis crisis linked to the deaths of several consumers of Maple Leaf Foods products, Michael refused to hide behind professionally groomed spokespersons. Initially against his lawyer's advice, he spoke openly and candidly to the public and speedily accepted full responsibility on behalf of the company for the outbreak. Michael insightfully states that "Accountability is different from responsibility. Responsibility is a direct link of 'I did that.' . . . Accountability exists for many, many things in life where we own the outcome even if it wasn't us who acted in a way that resulted in the outcome itself. Taking accountability begins with a deep, deep look in the mirror—in solitude, without the human natural instincts of defensiveness or deflection. Defensiveness and deflection are the enemies of genuine accountability. And this is a most important insight . . . it is better to hold ourselves accountable than it is to wait for others to hold us accountable. Rest assured, if or when we need to be held accountable, and we don't appear to be holding ourselves accountable, then others will do so in a much more material way than we ever would have ourselves!"[43]

Holding ourselves accountable means acknowledging the errors, accepting the consequences, making amends to those affected by the mistake and committing to an action plan to avoid making the same error again.

Risk and Correction: Sticking Your Neck Out

As I write this paragraph, the paperweight I am using to prevent the breeze from scattering my pages is the shape of a turtle. This pottery turtle reminds me of words attributed to Cecil Parker: "Behold the turtle. He only makes progress when he sticks his neck out." I realize that this is exactly what I did on the mountain. Once I reached the hut and realized the error in my plan, I had to correct my actions by sticking my neck out and attempting something different.

Admitting mistakes or changing behaviours does not always feel natural or comfortable, because it involves taking risk and experiencing vulnerability. Risk involves fear—fear of failure, loss, criticism, embarrassment or pain. The "size" of your fear in relation to the vision you seek determines the size of risk you are willing to take. Taking a risk is not about the absence of fear; rather, it is about the passion of your vision. Passion enables you to face your fear and do it anyway. After all, pushing through fear is less frightening than living with the fear that comes from feeling helpless. Almost everyone feels fear when approaching something new in life, yet so many go out there and attempt new things despite the fear, so we must conclude that *fear is not the problem*. The real issue has to do with how we perceive the fear. For some, the fear is irrelevant; for others, it creates a state of paralysis. The former perceive their fear from a position of power (that is, they embrace having a choice, which gives them energy and spurs them to action);

the latter hold it from a position of pain (that is, they feel help-less and depressed in the face of it, which paralyzes them). Per-ceiving fear from a power position requires tapping into the superconscious mind or a higher power.

In *Risk & Other Four-Letter Words,* Walter Wriston, former chairman of Citibank, states, "Play it safe; if there was ever a prescription for producing a dismal future, that has to be it." To escape the tedium of mediocrity and move in the direction of our dreams, we *must* take risks—calculated, deliberate and faith-filled risks. Peter Drucker, one of the most prolific writ-ers in the management and leadership field, has suggested that people who do not take risks make, on average, two big mistakes a year. People who *do* take risks make, on average, two big mistakes a year. So what do you have to lose?

Risk requires taking responsibility for your leadership choices. It is to trust and believe in the face of possibility despite not being able to know the outcome ahead of time. Leadership also demands being ready to take risks for the predicted benefits of followers, not neces-sarily yourself. Is this

> People who do not take risks make, on average, two big mistakes a year. People who *do* take risks make, on average, two big mistakes a year.

comfortable? No, of course not! The successful leader recog-nizes the value of, and makes use of, the "discomfort zone."

The comfort zone is one of the most difficult obstacles for leaders to overcome. It is powered by your unconscious urging you to remain consistent with what you have said and done in the past and, therefore, with the resultant habits that enslave you. When you risk adopting new behaviours—thinking, saying or doing things contrary to your current habits—your homeostatic impulse attempts to pull you back into your comfort zone by making you feel uneasy. While this impulse is normal and nature's way of keeping you consistent, all growth and progress (and, in my case, survival) requires the leader to move out of the comfort zone in the direction of something that will be more effective. If we succumb to the impulse not to change, we risk something altogether different. Remember Einstein's definition of insanity? "Doing the same thing over and over again and expecting different results."

Leadership development, growth, advancement, improvement, promotions, improved results, better performance and increased income all follow solely on the heels of new behaviour, which, by definition, is uncomfortable because of its unfamiliarity. I am not cursing when I say, "Thank God for discomfort. Thank God for adversity. Thank God for problems. Thank God for crises!" Leaders can learn from mistakes, from crises and from failures if they correct and adopt the attitude and practice of *correction-centred leadership*.

Next time you are given difficult feedback or when you fear change, try the following:

- Take a few five-second intervals to *step back and assess* the need to change. Pause and spend some time processing the information before you respond. Taking it all in at once can be overwhelming. Harness your *intuition* by quietly reflecting, praying or journaling your thoughts. This will help you identify what feedback is accurate versus what is perception and will also help you determine any changes you need to make. Be true and honest with yourself and your feelings as you assess the feedback or change ahead. Once you gauge the need for change, you can break down the actions needed to achieve the specific goal.

- Paint a picture in your mind of the outcome the change will yield. *Envision* how it will make you a better or more successful person or improve the company you are working on behalf of.

- *Speak truthfully to yourself* to give the change momentum and to support your progress. Tell yourself (out loud!) that you "are successful" and that you "can change," and *believe* that you can make the necessary changes. Our thoughts control our actions. Catch your mind if it tells you otherwise, and feed it with truth.

- *Have faith.* Your spiritual beliefs can help you find wisdom, peace and healing. God's grace has enabled changes I believe I could not have accomplished on my own. Believe in and trust your family or team at work, and seek their support through the change.

- Practise *authenticity* and *integrity* by not just outwardly discussing or planning the change to impress others but by actually changing. Believe in what you are doing—it will show in your actions.

If you are working to make changes in your character, make sure the changes are exercised both at home and at work.

- Ensure the change is rooted in your *habits*. Continue to repeat and reflect on the new behaviour or change. This will make it more difficult to slip back into old ways. Habit will help you be an authentic leader because it firmly roots the change within you or within your organization.

I will never forget the first time I drove with a GPS. I was heading out of town with my friends Jan and Mike. As we got in the car, Jan sighed and explained that after considerable negotiating, Mike had exchanged the food processor they'd received as a wedding gift (and which took up too much counter space) for this small and, according to Jan, "useless" device. Nevertheless, Jan turned the GPS on and, sure enough, made a few wrong turns. The GPS confidently stated, "Recalculating," and then directed us down a different street that still led to the desired destination. After that ride, Jan became a big fan of the GPS and her husband loved hearing the words, "You were right—this is better than a food processor." Let's think like a GPS next time we make a mistake. Realize and admit that you took a wrong turn, "recalculate," and take a different path to your desired destination.

TAKE FIVE SECONDS

Points to Ponder
Correction begins with accountability.
Accountability begins by looking in the mirror without defensiveness or deflection.

Quotes to Remember
"If we want to change the situation, we first have to change ourselves. And to change ourselves effectively, we first have to change our perceptions."
—*Stephen Covey*

"Any man whose errors take ten years to correct is quite a man."
—*J. Robert Oppenheimer, speaking of Albert Einstein*

"Consider how hard it is to change yourself, and you will understand what little chance you have of changing others." —*Jacob B. Braude*

"Success is going from failure to failure without loss of enthusiasm." —*Winston Churchill*

Questions to Consider
What feedback have I been given from others recently? What should I work on correcting in my character? For what life or career changes do I need to prepare myself?

8

PULLING BACK YOUR HAND
AUTHENTICITY AND INTEGRITY

"Ignore what they say about ethics; observe what they do."
—*Mark Pastin*

I vividly remember the horror I felt as I watched Bruce sliding down the mountain from above me. The only thing I could do to try to save him was outstretch my arm for him to grab. As our hands were about to meet, our eyes connected. Bruce pulled his hand back and continued the fall that ended his life. Had Bruce not pulled back his hand, his velocity most certainly would have taken me down the mountain with him. This moment of decision was a split second. Bruce did not have time to think about acting with integrity—he just did. I can't imagine a better example of authenticity; Bruce truly connected his hand with his heart in this act of love. Leaders, whether parents, spouses, teachers or managers, accomplish what is among the most difficult of things to do—they connect their hands with their hearts, their actions with their ethics, their walk with their talk.

Here's a tough question: Would you have pulled back your hand?

The majority of us would claim that we are ethical and authentic leaders. If another person questioned our integrity, we would probably take offence and almost certainly be keen to defend our honour, position and actions. But all of us can benefit from an in-depth examination of our personal standards of conduct and the degree to which we really live up to them. Will you feel good about mastering the seemingly impossible if you walk over others or neglect those you love along the way? What is the cost of the dream you are trying to realize?

Authenticity and integrity are paramount to goal accomplishment, especially if you want to elicit trust and followership. We must have the courage to turn the spotlight on our own core actions and habits if we are to be authentic leaders who can make positive differences in the lives of others as well as in our own. Authenticity is complex, so let's look more closely at defining authenticity and related concepts.

Values

Values are the criteria (standards or principles) by which we make judgments or choices and establish priorities. These values may include ethics; however, not all values reflect ethical rights and wrongs. For example, we may value a car or leisure, but these are not necessarily ethical values. Values could also be determined by our attitudes toward what we like and dislike.

Morals and Ethics

A subset of values, morals deal with rights and wrongs. Morality, derived from the Latin word *mores*, refers to generally accepted behaviours or customs often expressed in law. Morals reflect judgments made according to perceived standards of good or evil. Those who rely on the law as their standard of morality often forget that laws change. Laws can also be bent, dodged and misinterpreted. Furthermore, laws, because they are made by imperfect people, cannot be perfect in all situations or at all times.

The word ethics derives from the Greek word *ethos*, meaning root or foundation. Ethics represent the universal principles sustaining a particular morality. Ethics are not merely rules that are enforceable or justifiable but, rather, the appropriate application of morals to a particular situation.

Integrity

The Canadian Oxford Dictionary offers as the meanings of *integrity* "moral uprightness; honesty" and "wholeness; completeness." People with strong integrity act in concert with who they are on the inside. When a person has integrity, there is a thread of consistency among his or her values, morals, ethics and actions. Managers with integrity, for example, are consistent in word and deed and therefore invite trust from others. Integrity requires the capacity to resist attractive alternative actions that compromise principles and the capacity to assume risks in defence of these principles. Integrity for a leader is not a simple, unidimensional concept but rather a multifaceted process that operates at many levels: intra-personal, interpersonal, inter-group, organizational and societal.

Personal Integrity

Personal integrity requires operating with consistency in various settings and roles (for example, at work or home or in social settings; with managers, employees or customers). As long as we believe leaders are true to their sincerely held ethical principles, we do not question their personal integrity. We raise questions about a person's integrity, however, when we think that the person's behaviour is inconsistent with his or her personal visions of goodness or rightness.

As leaders, we need to be careful of the "bottom line" or "results" mentality. Winning or losing is not the only thing at stake—colleagues are not opponents; customers are not just sources of money. Successful talent-building companies measure their people's performance by both results and integrity, recognizing that a balance of both is essential to success and career development. For example, Jack Welch, former CEO of General Electric, lists two of the six criteria for promoting senior executives as honesty and integrity.

Social and Organizational Integrity

Social integrity requires consistency between action and principle but also adherence to generally accepted principles and standards of goodness or rightness of human conduct. When we raise questions about a person's social integrity, we are questioning whether his or her behaviour is consistent with reasonable and appropriate moral principles.

"A house or kingdom divided against itself cannot stand" (Mark 3:24, NIV). To gain trust and respect, an organization's policies and practices must also be consistent with its espoused beliefs. As simple as this may seem, within a number of organizations, there nonetheless often appear to be "integrity gaps" between stated values and business practices. For example, an organization may publicly claim, "Our people are our most valued asset," and yet do little to ensure that employees receive career planning, coaching and performance appraisals.

> An organization may claim, "Our people are our most valued asset," and yet do little to ensure that employees receive coaching and performance appraisals.

A company may well value "empowerment, trust, equality and dignity for all" yet offer different classes of travel for various levels of employees or special parking lots for vice-presidents. A company may preach that it supports work–life balance while its senior leaders regularly can be found in their offices until late in the evening or sending multiple emails on the weekends. When these types of gaps exist, not only the integrity but also the credibility of and respect for the organization and its management simply evaporate. Take, for example, John Thain, CEO of Merrill Lynch. In 2008, when the company was facing a US$15-billion fourth-quarter loss and struggling to rein in expenses, Thain approved the ultra-luxurious $1.2-million renovation of his own office and suggested that he deserved a US$10-million bonus. (Amidst the US mortgage crisis, most other top executives were volunteering to forgo their bonuses.) A management professor at Boston University responded, "It's the kind of self-indulgence that often bespeaks of poor judgment and a disregard to what's happening to other people in the organization, much less investors."[43] Thain was subpoenaed by New York's Attorney General and is part of a larger investigation into firms that paid out big bonuses while accepting billions of dollars in bailout money from taxpayers.

Authenticity

Integrity is the foundation of authenticity; however, authenticity moves one step beyond integrity. Authenticity is integrity in its most genuine state. Authenticity means that when the mask is peeled off, you are acting in the way you really want to. Commitment to the truth establishes an internal rapport and the deep level of congruence that reflects a leader's real character. Whereas integrity is doing the right thing to achieve the best result, authenticity is the actual belief and heart that truly *wants* to do the right thing and would do it even if no one were watching. Bruce demonstrated authenticity when he pulled back his hand to save my life.

Authenticity is the soul of business and leadership. For example, if you sell something you genuinely believe in, people will trust you. Authenticity is the heart making the sale; trust is the heart making the purchase. Imagine going to an electronics store to purchase a TV and the salesperson recommending something less expensive than the model you initially had in mind. This salesperson would have clearly invested time listening to your needs, explained all the options including their pros and cons and, based on what you value, made a recommendation. The salesperson didn't use this technique because it was a best practice but because he or she genuinely wanted to help you. How would you feel? Most likely you would return to that same salesperson (or store) the next time because he or she gained your trust and recommended the right product for you without concern for his or her commission. Similarly, teachers who genuinely "sell" the topic they are teaching by showing a passion to helping people learn have a stronger impact on students. Likewise, managers who genuinely believe in their people and who would be committed to developing them even if the boss wasn't watching have a stronger impact on employees. The heart of successful leadership pulses from authenticity.

Authentic leaders inspire, cultivate and spread the spirit of authenticity throughout their home or organization. A "well-ordered soul," living by and consistently applying such ground rules, is the essence of personal authentic leadership. Opportunity and advantage too easily displace integrity when we are not up to addressing the soul-searching complexity that authenticity calls for. You can't bluff people for long. Behind the mask, who are you? What are you really thinking? What do you truly believe in? Many have learned that the serenity of being alone, surrounded by the quietness of nature and nothing but their own breath, allows for true distillation of who they are and who they want to become. One characteristic of authentic leaders is that they make quiet time to reflect on their thoughts and actions. They take five seconds to pause and breathe.

To give an analogy, as we learn to drive a car, the specific procedures are at first individual tasks that we have to consciously think about, but they increasingly become automatic. Gradually, driving becomes so much a part of our "natural" functioning that we become explicitly aware of it only when we take time to reflect upon our actions. However, without *knowing* the procedure, we would find it impossible to drive. Similarly, without a clear knowledge of our values, beliefs and principles, it is impossible to make consistent and sound decisions about what is valuable and what ways are acceptable in achieving what is valuable.

The Impact of Time on Authenticity

Time pressures can derail even our deepest convictions about integrity. This is a very real danger in a culture that often tells us that we are late or that there is more to do. The "rush, rush, do, do" mentality and drive to achieve our goals can distract us from demonstrating authenticity and integrity.

John M. Darley and C. Daniel Batson conducted an interesting study of students at Princeton Theological Seminary to examine helping behaviour. Some participants were to give a talk about jobs in which seminary students would be most effective; others were to speak about the parable of the Good

Samaritan. After an initial survey, participants were directed to a lab in the building next door. On arrival, some of the students were told, "Uh-oh, you're late! They were expecting you a few minutes ago. The assistant should be waiting for you, so you'd better hurry." Other students were told, "The assistant is ready for you, so please go right over." And still others were told, "It'll be a few minutes before they're ready for you, but you might as well head on over. It shouldn't be long."

While in transit, each student passed a slumped "victim" planted in a doorway in an alleyway outside. The victim, his head down and eyes closed, was not moving. As each student walked by, the victim coughed twice and groaned, keeping his head down. The "victim" then secretly rated each seminary student on his helping behaviour. Forty per cent of the students offered some form of direct or indirect aid to the victim; 60 per cent did not. The degree of hurry the student was in correlated negatively to his helping behaviour. In addition, the study found that those who were going to speak about the parable of the Good Samaritan were not significantly more likely to stop than those who were going to talk about possible occupations for seminary graduates—thus inadvertantly confirming the point of the parable. (Indeed, several students going to give a talk on this parable literally *stepped over* the victim as they hurried on their way!) The study concluded that people who are not in a hurry may stop and offer help to a person in distress, but those in a hurry are likely to keep going. The authors of the study stated, "It is difficult not to conclude . . . that ethics become a luxury as the speed of our daily lives increases."[45]

The lesson is clear. *Comprehending* moral values does not ensure acting upon them. Mastery over ethics and integrity does not guarantee leaders mastery over themselves. Tyrannized by time, leaders can inadvertently overlook the anguish of others—the despondent colleague with the drinking problem, the harassed salesperson struggling to reach impossible quotas, the distressed employee with an ailing spouse, a family member who needs love.

On Mount Ruapehu, I internalized the value of time. Five seconds seemed like eternity when all of the noise of life was removed. For me, five seconds was enough time to perish. In a paradigm in which time is money and money is considered god, we need to stop and reflect on how we spend our time. How we spend our time is a good indication of what is truly authentic to us. In a sixteen-hour day, assuming eight hours are spent sleeping, there are 11,520 five-second intervals! How many of these five-second intervals do you spend encouraging others? How many do you spend on *quality* family time? Watching TV does not count.

Shrinking the Authenticity Gap

Achieving authenticity and integrity first requires shrinking the gap between our walk and our talk. This includes the gap between our personal and professional lives. Leaders at all levels are facing increasing and recurring tension between organizational commitment and personal obligations. Long hours, or frequent business trips, separate people from their families and communities. Perhaps the most insidious evil is take-home work because, if a common occurrence, it can make people unavailable to their spouses and children. A subtle ruthlessness can easily evolve, and the consequences become plain to see. Leaders may own their own homes but act like tenants, live in middle-class suburbs but know no neighbours and enjoy large incomes but possess small wealth. In a moment of reflective openness, I too have soberly asked, "By trying to achieve my goals, do I work for the good life or do I live for a good work?" and "Am I a human being or am I a human doing?" A common defence for workaholic tendencies is, "I do it for the family." Yet, are your spouse's or children's needs being ignored? The saddest leaders are those who have lulled themselves into believing that their zeal for the job justifies any burden they foist upon others.

It is possible and disturbingly easy for a leader to devote in excess of twelve hours per day, six days a week, to the thousands of people, projects and passions out there and still not have a deep meaningful relationship with his or her spouse, own children and closest working associates. It takes more nobility of character, courage, strength and humility to rebuild one special relationship than it does to devote hundreds of hours to those masses of people, causes and projects. As difficult and uncomfortable as it is, acknowledging the workaholic trap that leaders so easily fall prey to is a critical aspect of authenticity and integrity. The leader who wishes to be credible, respected and trustworthy has no option other than to look very closely at his or her innermost core. Leaders must clean up their nets before they can be fishers of men, teams, departments, organizations or nations.

Duplicity (for example, a gap between heart and hands, private and public, words and actions) is probably the surest way for a leader to lose power and potential as a change agent within any organization. Besides, what does a person really profit by gaining the world but losing his or her own self? Duplicity generates distrust: A duplicitous person's so-called good human relations techniques will be perceived as manipulation. In our heart of hearts, we can all testify to the truth of the saying "You reap what you sow."

The CN Tower in Toronto, standing 1,815 feet tall, contains 53,000 cubic yards of concrete.[46] Of that huge volume of concrete, more than 35,406 cubic yards are underground, forming the foundation (or bedrock) that no one sees. The tower—which serves as a communication tower, receiving and sending messages across North America and beyond—is an appropriate symbol for a leader who wishes to personify a communication beacon across his or her organization, country or even world. Our power comes from our character—the part of our makeup that is "below ground." Leaders can establish themselves as communication towers and believe they are operating as effective change agents yet never approach "CN Tower capacity" because of their failure to deal with one or two relationships at the heart of their professional and personal lives. The more I study and work with various organizations, the more I discover that problems within an organization often stem from relationship difficulties among those within the upper executive—between partners or owners, between a CEO and his or her executive VP, and so on.

I am convinced that as a prerequisite to our attempts to shrink the "gap," we must gain a clearer sense of our personal values, beliefs, principles and *purpose*—the part of us that is "underground." There is a critical difference between a leader's goal and his or her purpose. A goal is a target, something to shoot for, and no longer exists once it is hit or missed. A purpose, on the other hand, is a way of being or function- ing and is viewed as valuable in itself. A purpose is a particu- lar road a leader chooses to travel, whereas a goal is one of the places he or she intends to visit along that road. Purposes persist. The leader with integrity stands on his or her pur- pose, consulting it as a foundation, as an assurance that his or her decisions and actions have meaning. To understand the difference between goals and purpose, we can consider that citing company goals answers the question, "Where is the company headed, and when does it intend to be there?" Conversely, citing company purposes answers the question, "Why is the existence of this organization worthwhile, and why should I perform this task or seek this company's goals with maximum commitment?" Purpose within an organiza- tion provides a sense of what it is, where its goals come from and why trying hard matters. I see huge opportunity in the fact that "when asked what they do for a living, most people describe the tasks they perform every day, not the *purpose* of the greater enterprise in which they take part."[47]

Leaders can begin shrinking the authenticity gap by prob- ing their basic values and articulating their personal answers to these questions:

- What do I see as my fundamental purpose in life?
- Are people basically self-seeking, or are they basi- cally good and generous?
- Do people have a transcendental and spiritual end, or is this present life with its pleasures and material satisfactions all there is?

- Is there such a thing as a moral absolute, or is everything relative?
- Does society exist for people, or do people exist for society?
- What are the personal values I stand behind?
- What are the values of the company I work for?
- How can I spend my energy in a manner that is consistent with my values?[48]

Authentic Leaders Serve Others

"Servant leadership" presents the paradox that greatness comes from exercising humility. Authentic leaders must inwardly define their actions as neither power trips nor gamesmanship but rather as servanthood—that is, as making a contribution to the good of the organization, home or society in which they perform the action. Which of the following behaviours of "servant leaders" can you model?

- Servant leaders are leaders second and teachers first.
- Servant leaders have a great capacity for listening and they give help even when it's not their job.
- Servant leaders give credit for others' ideas and build on their people's strengths and contributions.
- Servant leaders genuinely strive to enhance their people and unlock their talents, not to have their own perceived greatness endorsed.
- Servant leaders work to provide the support necessary for their team to succeed.
- Servant leaders look for the good and positive in others and acknowledge when they find it.

- Servant leaders have empathy and always accept the person, even if they don't accept the person's behaviour or performance.

Connecting Our Hearts with Our Hands

What we are communicates our character far more eloquently than does what we say, and it is only when our words are fully congruent with what we are that we have the power, credibility and followership necessary to lead and develop others. In his bestselling book *Leadership Jazz*, Max DePree shares a personal story about a nurse's instructions for his immediate role with his newborn granddaughter. Born prematurely, the baby weighed one pound seven ounces and was so small, Max says, that a wedding ring could slide up her arm to her shoulder. The baby's father had taken off a month before her birth. Deeming Max the surrogate father, the nurse advised him to continually tell his granddaughter how much he loved her while simultaneously stroking the child's body with the tips of his fingers. She said, "She has to be able to connect your voice to your touch." [49] Similarly, all followers need to be able to connect their leaders' voices (talk) to their actions (walk) and their hands (actions) to their hearts (character).

My fervent hope is that this chapter will create a "positive disturbance" for you, inspiring you to slow down despite the high-velocity culture that often characterizes our modern world. Please take the necessary time to reflect on the ideas presented. I am encouraged that Maple Leaf Foods participants took the time to reflect after attending one of my workshops. They wrote in appreciation, "We now feel that anything is possible, that the means to achieve self-awareness and self-actualization is *within* each of us and that through direct personal leadership we *will* be eagles, we *will* seize the moment, and we *will* impact the teams we lead and the company we serve. You taught us that 'We are what we *think* we are,' and we now know that '*How* we lead is *who* we are.' You lead in what I personally believe is the most powerful way to lead—and that's by example. The vulnerability, trust and love you shared with us was nothing short of exemplary!"

Commit yourself to your own personal mastery of identifying, examining and, if need be, modifying your own character, as many of my students have done. As J.R.R. Tolkien wisely said, "Deep roots are not reached by the frost." Rooting integrity into your habits is the most powerful way to become an authentic leader. We will discuss habits in the next chapter.

Take Five Seconds

Point to Ponder
Walking your talk reflects integrity; believing in your talk reflects authenticity.

Quotes to Remember
"The man of integrity walks securely."
—*Proverbs 10:19*

"No action of management has more impact on its operational ethics than the people it promotes, dismisses or allows to stagnate." —*Ronald R. Sims*

"What is needed more than anything else in management and government is the well-ordered soul."
—*Barbara Tuchman*

"The leader's first task is to be the trumpet that sounds a clear sound." —*Peter Drucker*

Question to Consider
How can you shrink the duplicity in your own personal and professional life?

9

WE ARE WHAT WE REPEATEDLY DO
HABIT

"We are what we repeatedly do.
Excellence, then, is not an act but a habit."
—*Aristotle*

It is appropriate that habit-centred leadership be presented as the last bedrock underlying successful leadership because the stepping stones discussed thus far are dependent upon the pivotal importance of this principle. It is vital to recognize that we are slaves to our habits. Successful leaders have successful habits. Unsuccessful leaders do not. My habits saved my life on Mount Ruapehu. If I hadn't established such habits, each survival technique I attempted to use might have failed, and I would not have achieved the seemingly impossible.

What is a habit? A habit is simply a behaviour that you consistently repeat. Taking your shoes off when entering a home is an example of a habit—it is something that has become second nature to you. Habit is rooted in who you are as a person. As we pause to reflect, we will recognize not only that are we creatures of habit but also that our normal daily activities are, by and large, routines. Consider yesterday, and I would guarantee that there are hundreds of things you did the same way as you did them the day before and the day before that: the way you dress, eat breakfast (or not), prepare for the day, clean your teeth (or not), greet people at work, arrange your desk, answer the phone, turn on your computer and so forth. A study using a large sample of RCMP officers reported that, on average, men shave with an identical pattern of strokes, give or take only two movements, each day.

Because we are creatures of habit, unless we consciously change our behaviour, we will always eat the same food, earn the same amount of money, associate with the same people, drive the same car and read the same types of books. Newton's first law of motion cements this truth: A body at rest tends to remain at rest and a body in motion tends to remain in motion unless acted upon by an outside force. Our thinking and leadership behaviour are subject to the same law. In the absence of an outside force or a definite decision upon our part to do something differently, we will keep on doing the same thing indefinitely.

Habits That Will Help You Accomplish the Impossible

Habit One: Reflection

I got through the night on Mount Ruapehu by breathing in and warming the air, then breathing out and counting "one, two, three, four, five." I gave thanks for getting through those five seconds and then repeated the practice. By default, my personality goes into panic or stress mode when faced with a large obstacle. Knowing this, I trained myself in the habit of stepping back and breaking down large tasks or challenges into smaller pieces so that I wouldn't get overwhelmed. Thank goodness I had practised this habit for some time prior to the climb.

Once you establish what your "big rocks" are, you too can break them down into more realistic bites. Each bite should contain specific tasks and timelines within which to accomplish the goal. Setting realistic expectations of yourself and prioritizing in light of the big rocks are cornerstones to the effectiveness of Five Seconds at a Time. The application of this technique naturally requires deliberate thought and planning on the part of the leader. He or she must assess the time and resources required to reach a goal and determine where that goals fits in reference to other priorities. However, the Five Seconds at a Time technique can be applied to immediate challenges as well. If you feel as if you are in crisis mode or feel too overwhelmed to begin a task, stop, take a step back and pause. Breathe and take five seconds to regroup and refocus. Identify what you can do in the next five minutes or even in the next few hours to overcome small parts of the challenge. Remember that a journey that seems like a thousand miles begins with but one step and that by taking a series of small steps, you will achieve milestones in the journey. People who accomplish great feats recognize that the human in human being is built to need rest and renewal. Remember to incorporate time to pause, reflect and celebrate.

Habit Two: Vision

I accomplished the seemingly impossible, in part, by pausing, praying, planning and repeatedly rehearsing how each footstep would be placed once I left the safety of a de-iced rock. Envisioning my survival and helicopter rescue before it happened provided hope and encouragement to keep on going.

Envisioning is a powerful habit that allows leaders to focus ahead of time on what they want to achieve. Attaching a purpose to your vision will help it live in your heart and thoughts. Like the pianist who accomplished the seemingly impossible feat of improving his skill without physically playing, practise vividly in your mind and watch yourself hit each note successfully. When you make a mistake, rewind and attempt the note again until you get it right. Train yourself habitually to think of the possibilities by asking yourself, "What if?" Listen to your intuition, using it as a sounding board for your vision.

Habit Three: Intuition

My habit of being still and listening to my inner thoughts and promptings saved my life. My intuition guided me to climb back up the mountain. If I had continued down the mountain, I almost assuredly would have frozen to death without the shelter of the hut to block the wind. In my own personal leadership journey, I have found my intuition to be closely linked to my faith—a guiding hand leading my path.

Effective leaders generally acknowledge that when possible, fact finding and evaluation should precede intuition in decision making. Intuition is a powerful habit when used as a "gut check" before making the final

> If we challenge ourselves regularly to step back, reflect and ask, "Does this choice *feel* right?" before taking the next step, we are starting to build an intuitive habit.

call. In this fast-paced life, it is easy just to keep our heads down, methodically checking things off the list. If we challenge ourselves regularly to step back, reflect and ask, "Does this choice feel right?" before taking the next step, we are starting to build an intuitive habit. Regularly paying attention to what is going on inside (your energy, blocks, inner dialogues or instincts) will help you accomplish the seemingly impossible. Be open if your intuition leads you down a different path than you initially planned to take. Building awareness of your own intuition will help you unlock creativity and better understand your gifts and talents of brilliance.

Habit Four: Positive Thought Choice

I am convinced that I am alive today because of my *learned habit to locate the blessing in every circumstance*. A month of training my mind to seek the good has enabled me to look for blessings habitually, even in adversity. Even when I ice-axed my way into the hut and was hit with the agonizing realization that it didn't house any means of my immediately getting help, my habitually positive mind sought out the beer can and toboggan liner as objects of hope, encouragement and positive expectation. My habit of talking to myself out loud paid off handsomely as my monologues helped me slow down and contemplate alternatives with a peace and calmness of mind, enabling appropriate decision making. Panicking or succumbing to despair would have likely paralyzed my mind as well as my body. I find that talking to myself out loud gives me a sense of control, clarity and confidence.

Although we can't always have power over our feelings, by choosing to control our thoughts, we can control our attitude toward situations. This perspective is vital to leaders' accomplishing the seemingly impossible. Successful leaders understand that attitude is more important than knowledge or skill. Thus, our thoughts are pivotal to our success. Controlling your thoughts and filling your mind with uplifting talk will have an impact on not only your success but also your overall happiness. Expect success and make it a habit!

Habit Five: Faith and Action

My habit of *trusting* in God, especially during times of trouble, allowed me to let go of my anxiety and find peace during the longest night of my life. I got into the wheelbarrow. My faith enabled me to believe that I could reach the hut even when the reality of the ice wall was most vivid—and intimidating. Without faith, I would not have had the confidence or will to keep going.

Faith can mean different things to different people. Regardless of whether or not you are religious, the habits of faith, belief and trust enable action. Faith gives leaders the courage to keep moving forward, even when part of the path ahead is unknown. Believing in your team (employees, family and yourself) builds confidence, and trusting them enables you to delegate so that you can bring others onboard to help you in achieving your goals.

Habit Six: Correction

The habit of continually correcting my mistakes instead of dwelling on them also contributed to saving my life on Mount Ruapehu. I realized I had made a mistake once I entered the hut and found it drained of all supplies. Because I had trained my mind to focus on correction in the face of an error, rather than on regret, I automatically took corrective measures and began to create a survival plan using the few items I found in the hut.

We all make mistakes. Developing the habit of beginning, acting and correcting is imperative to reaching your dreams. Correction requires self-awareness and a willingness to be accountable for your actions. Admitting mistakes is neither easy nor comfortable and may feel risky at first. Think of an obstacle not as a roadblock but rather as an opportunity to learn and to attempt something different.

Habit Seven: Authenticity and Integrity

Bruce is my role model for both authenticity and integrity. He had only a split second to make the decision to pull back his hand, proving that integrity was rooted in his character. Authenticity is the belief and heart that truly wants to do the right thing, even if no one is watching. Authenticity reveals who you really are behind the mask.

The challenge for leaders is consistently to connect their hands to their hearts, their actions to their values and their walk to their talk. In your quest to accomplish your goals and dreams, make sure you ask, "At what cost?" Consider whether, once you've achieved your goal, you'll be comfortable in your own skin. Be mindful of how you prioritize your time with your family and friends.

How to Change Bad Habits and Form Good Ones

Changing habits that are no longer consistent with your higher purpose is one of the hardest things you will ever do—but it is essential to improving the quality of your life and your leadership. Unless you have already actively done the work necessary for reaching some level of excellence, you are living today with habits that you must discard if you are going to advance. Remember that bad habits are easy to form but hard to live with; good habits are hard to form but easy to live with.

Leadership development is a journey, not a destination, and as a result, there are always further stages of development and growth to challenge us. As we look deeply into the mirror, we all can find habits that are not constructive, positive or healthy. The encouraging news is that you can change negative consequences into positive outcomes and rewards simply by changing your habits—one behaviour at a time.

CHANGING YOUR HABITS

IDENTIFY negative habits.

ENVISION the benefits of forming new habits.

CREATE competing responses.

ALTER your environment.

REPEAT AND PRACTISE desired behaviours.

Identify Negative Habits

All habits are the result of our previous conditions. They are things we learn to do and then practise until they not only become automatic but seem natural ways to behave. They are, of course, not natural at all—we weren't born with any of them. They are habits—programs that stuck. The trick is to identify the negative habits that undermine your leadership success and replace them with positive ones. The most dangerous habits you can form are mental habits. Because whatever you think about continually, you create in your life; your negative or self-limiting thoughts hurt you more than almost any other activity you can engage in. Consider asking family members and/or colleagues to share their observations of your bad habits. (It is humbling to remember that it is our outward behaviour that reflects the truth of who we are; our perceptions are often illusions and rationalizations.) How do your negative habits affect your personal life, family life, social life or professional life? The exercises at the back of this book will help you further assess your habits.

Envision the Benefits of Forming New Habits

What are the benefits of overcoming negative habits? These benefits could apply to your personal, family, social or professional life. For example, if you have a habit of complaining, the personal benefit of adopting an attitude of thankfulness could be stress relief or increased happiness. Envision what your life would be like without the weight of this habit. Envision how you would look, act and relate to others. How does this make you feel? As discussed in Chapter 3, keep your sights on the point at which you want to arrive. The things we give our attention to are amplified, therefore what we envision and focus on is crucial. The more vividly you envision the benefits of adopting new behaviours, the easier it is to take action (and the more likely you are to do so).

Create a Competing Response

Experts in habit change have found *competing responses* and self-talk to be effective tools in helping to change habits. A competing response is an alternative behaviour to the negative habit. For example, if your habit is biting your fingernails, your competing response could be putting your hands in your pockets. The competing response should not be compatile with the habit and should require "little response effort."[50]

Imagine yourself in a situation that provokes a habit that you want to change. Now envision yourself starting your competing response instead of employing your habit. Engaging in self-talk while you are mentally envisioning this process can also help solidify change. As discussed in Chapter 5, habit-changing self-talk directs your subconscious mind to stop doing something in one way and to start doing it in another. It is important to rehearse by envisioning your competing response and vividly imagining yourself successfully overcoming your habit.

Alter Your Environment

What tempts you to engage in the negative habit? Is there a certain time, place, feeling or pattern associated with it? Brainstorm ways you can take this temptation out of your life. For example, if your negative habit is eating junk food before bed, you could either stop keeping junk food in the house or ask a family member to hide the junk food and let you have only a moderate amount after dinner, and not before bed.

Repeat and Practise Desired Behaviours

It is well recognized that if you persist in any new behaviour, it eventually becomes automatic. Continual practice of a musical instrument, like the saxophone, allows the brain automatically to correlate the notes on the manuscript to the correct fingering on the instrument—it takes practice and habit formation to play beautiful music. It is important to note that simply "dabbling" in new behaviours will not establish habits. Of course, self-discipline is necessary for constructive habit formation. The good news is that you can reprogram yourself anytime you choose to do so.

However, your habits cannot be created—or changed—by anyone else but you! Aristotle, one of the greatest philosophers of all time, defines habit as a firm disposition of human power. It takes human willpower to change the nature of habits. As further motivation to repeat and practise desired behaviours, Aristotle teaches that we can be truly happy only when good habits become rooted in who we are as humans. Success and failure, happiness and unhappiness, are largely the results of habits.

To remain realistic, we must remember that there are no quick fixes. A new behaviour will not become automatic without at least twenty-five repetitions. (Some writers report that at least thirty repetitions are required before a habit is established.) But ultimately, "when behaviour is performed many times, one does not need to weigh pros and cons or to check one's attitudes and behavioural control in order to arrive at a choice. . . . Habit strength increases as a result of repetitions of positive reinforcements."[51]

You Can Change!
Write down the new behaviour and the concrete steps you will take to accomplish it; this may sound simple enough, but 97 per cent of the world does not do it!

- *Identify* a new desired habit (e.g., eating less junk food).
- *Envision* and then write down and say aloud the benefits of forming the new habit (e.g., feeling healthier and losing weight).
- *Create a competing response* to the old habit (e.g., snacking on something healthy when you crave junk food).
- Brainstorm ways to *alter your environment* (e.g., throwing away all junk food in the house and stocking cupboard with healthy snacks).
- *Take action* by committing to twenty-five repetitions of the competing response.

In addition, the practice exercises at the end of this book contain some great tools to help you change your habits. And you can change them if you *want* to. Any thought or action you repeat often enough becomes a new habit. By disciplining yourself to think and to act in a way that is consistent with your new higher ideals and by doing this long enough for them to become new habits, you can develop into the kind of person, leader, partner or parent you want to be. Because your outer world corresponds to your inner world (thought objectification), as you begin to establish more constructive ways of thinking and behaving, people and situations around you will begin to change in remarkable yet predictable ways. Through good habits, you can accomplish what once seemed impossible. The habits of Five Seconds—Reflection, Vision, Intuition, Positive Thought Choice, Faith and Action, Correction, and Authenticity and Integrity—not only resulted in my survival on Mount Ruapehu but have also allowed me to accomplish many other challenging goals throughout my life. The automatic ways you respond and react to what is going on around you will determine the success of your journey. Don't attempt to change everything all at once but rather step by step—*Five Seconds at a Time.*

Take Five Seconds

Point to Ponder
Your mission is to establish good habits and make them your masters.

Quotes to Remember
"In the end, climbing is not about conquering the rock; it is about conquering yourself." —*Jim Collins*

"Habit is overcome by habit." —*Thomas à Kempis*

"There isn't anything that isn't made easier through constant familiarity and training." —*Dalai Lama*

"One moment after a man dies, he knows how he should have lived." —*Unknown*

Question to Consider
What habit(s) will I commit to changing?

EPILOGUE

*"What we call the beginning is often the end. And to make an end is
to make a beginning. The end is where we start from."*
—*T.S. Eliot*

Eliot's poetic words prompt me to end this book with an epilogue to the opening story. I am privileged to have a very special sister, Kathleen, who had enjoyed thirteen wonderful years of marriage to Bruce before he was tragically taken from us.

Kathleen was expectably devastated by her loss and still misses Bruce tremendously. She spent considerable time "stepping back" in reflection and healing. Equally understandable is the fact that Mount Ruapehu, which is located quite close to where she still lives, represents a particularly painful memory of tragic loss. Can you guess what Kathleen did within a year of losing Bruce? She climbed that mountain.

What inspires me most is the reason Kathleen "stepped forward" to climb Mount Ruapehu. It wasn't to face the fears and hurts that the mountain had created for her (although she did that, too, which was an exceptionally courageous act); rather, she told me, "I climbed the mountain to stock the hut."

When I heard that, I burst into tears. She went on to explain that having it stocked with supplies would help any future climbers who found themselves in a predicament similar to the one I was in. What an inspirational testimony to her courage, compassion and integrity.

You may now understand why I placed Kathleen's name at the top of the list of those to whom I dedicate the book and why it seems appropriate now to end the text where I began. Yet there is a final acknowledgment to Kathleen's authentically lived habits of vision, intuition, thought choice, faith, correction and high level of love (similar to that of Bruce). On her way back down the mountain, she found the pack that had bounced off Bruce's body as he'd fallen at least 3,000 feet. When my rescuers found his body, thus allowing hundreds of his beloved friends to celebrate his truly inspiring life, they weren't even looking for the pack. Truthfully, no one really concerned themselves with the fact that the pack was not found. We'd found his body, and that was the main thing.

But Kathleen found the pack. Because it had been buried for months under snow and ice, the deep-freeze conditions had preserved the negatives of my camera. I shouldn't really have these shots, but Kathleen's courage and integrity enabled me to honour Bruce by displaying the last photograph of him, minutes before he fell, at the start of this book.

Thank you, Kathleen—you are a walking miracle and the best sister anyone could ask for!

PUTTING IT ALL INTO PRACTICE

We wish you success in realizing your full potential, both personally and professionally, with the aid of this book. To that end, we have included questions for reflection and practical tools related to each chapter to assist you in translating the lessons of the story to your day-to-day life.

"Thoughts disentangle themselves when they pass through your fingertips."[52] We strongly encourage you to create a reading group to discuss each chapter's implications and applications to your life. Such a group can be powerful, as it allows for the exchange of information about what you are learning. This experience will ensure a dynamic journey of both self-reflection and community growing. Your group may choose to reflect on some questions individually and discuss others. As Winston Churchill taught, effective leaders are "approachable, accessible and vulnerable." Your authenticity and vulnerability in openly sharing will serve as a gift of learning for the rest of the group and a personal sounding board for you as you witness their encouragement and feedback. Ask each other questions such as "So what?" "What now?" and "How can this apply to my work or family?" Commit to each other in advance to consider these conversations confidential, listen to and encourage each other, and hold each other accountable by following up.

REFLECTION

1. What are the costs of anxiety and stress? How does being overwhelmed affect you? Check the box beside any of the items that apply. When life gets challenging or busy, do you

❑ set unrealistic goals?
❑ neglect your family?
❑ have emotional outbursts?
❑ treat people differently than you normally would?
❑ fail to see humour in situations?
❑ feel disorganized?
❑ start to disengage or not enjoy things that you normally would enjoy?
❑ neglect exercise or nutrition?
❑ sleep too little?
❑ have trouble focusing?
❑ feel helpless or depressed?
❑ forget to build breaks or relaxation into your day?
❑ feel as though you are running in circles?

❑ complain that there is too little time in the day?

❑ feel anxious and weighed down by everything on your plate?

❑ other?

2. How can the Five Seconds at a Time technique help you to step back and change your responses to stressful or challenging situations?

3. Reflect on a goal you've set for yourself but have not yet accomplished. Was this goal realistic? Was it SMART (specific, measurable, achievable, rewarded, time-limited)?

4. If you were to redefine this goal using what you learned from this chapter, how would you change it?

5. How many projects do you have on the go right now? Include projects both at work and outside of work. How can Little's Law (that less is more) help you reap results faster and more effectively?

6. What are your overall goals for this year? To visualize them, you can write these "big rocks" as "rock" pictures. Big rocks could relate to your job, volunteer work, family, health or a specific project. Using prioritization criteria, write numbers on the rocks to designate the importance of each.

7. On page 173 is an example of a prioritization matrix. Try using it to help you identify criteria for your big rocks and rank your priorities against them.

8. Pick one of your big rocks, identified in the question above—maybe the rock that you feel most overwhelmed by or your first-priority rock. Using the Five Seconds at a Time technique on page 21, step back and reflect and then break this goal or task into smaller components or stepping stones. Record the stepping stones in priority order.

9. Beside each step, record a date or time by which you will have accomplished it. Make sure this timeline is realistic.

10. What are your milestones? How will you reward yourself for achieving them?

11. Is there a situation in your life right now that makes you feel particularly overwhelmed? If so, I encourage you to step back and work through the following exercise. Then step forward by sharing this situation and your Five Seconds at a Time solution with your reading group.

CRITERIA IMPORTANT TO ME	Importance Weight	Taking Care of back problems	Score	Attending child's soccer game	Score	Working on project summit	Score	Getting to know colleagues	Score	Home move organization	Score
Personal enjoyment	5	5	25	5	25	1	5	3	15	1	5
Meeting manager expectations	5	0	0	0	0	5	25	1	5	0	0
Proactivity	1	3	3	3	3	3	3	3	3	3	3
Spending time with family	10	5	50	5	50	0	0	0	0	1	10
Personal Health	10	5	50	1	10	0	0	0	0	0	0
PRIORITY TOTAL			128		88		33		23		18

- First of all, create your own list of criteria and enter them in the left-hand column.
- Next, assign importance weights to each criterion (1=slightly important, 5=moderately important, 10=very important) and enter these in the second column.
- Now create your list of priorities (big rocks) and enter them in the top row.
- Rank the rocks according to how they meet the criteria, using the same weighting system as before.
- Multiply the criteria weight and the big rock rank to calculate the score for each rock.
- Add the scores in each column to calculate the total priority score.

Overwhelming Situation

Read through the following situation and pretend it is you facing the challenge. Use the Five Seconds at a Time principles to step back, reflect, identify the big rocks and break them down to make the situation seem less overwhelming. Use the questions as a guide. This exercise is particularly effective when done in a small group. Each group member should first work through the challenge individually and then share his or her solution with the team. A possible solution has been provided; however, before reading it, you should develop your own solution first.

Situation

It's Monday and it's your first day in a management position at a new company. Initially, you were assured your predecessor, Roy, would train you thoroughly. However, he had to take an emergency medical leave from work, so now you have to navigate the new job on your own. You feel dizzy as you look around at the extremely messy office with stacks of dusty paper everywhere. The floor-to-ceiling cabinets are jam-packed with papers with no apparent labelling system. You even have a hard time finding a piece of blank paper to write down requests from the numerous phone calls you have already received. Most of the calls are from people you have not yet met, and you have no idea what they are asking for. You notice the voice mail is still set up in Roy's name but haven't had time to change it. Your new boss, Suzan, seems extremely driven and expects results immediately. At ten o'clock, she bustles into your office and asks you to prepare an update on "Project Summit" by Friday. Naturally, you ask, "What is Project Summit?" She hastily replies, "I'm too busy to explain. Book an appointment with me to discuss further." Identifying that Suzan's time is hard to get, you use this window of opportunity to ask for a job description. Suzan responds, "I don't know where to find one. Check Roy's filing cabinet." Good luck, you think to yourself, as you again look at the ceiling-high wall-to-wall filing cabinet. In the back of your mind, you are thinking about your son Patrick's soccer championship game at six o'clock. Your back has been out of joint for a few days now (due to lifting boxes from your recent move), but you haven't had time to book an appointment with a massage therapist. Your aching back reminds you of the disarray at home— the many boxes still needing to be unpacked and the endless list of "fix-its" to be done. You have no idea where to find things at the office, let alone what you're doing. You feel anxious and stressed. Where do you start?

Questions

1. If it were you in this situation, how would you be feeling? What would you be thinking? Take some quiet time to just reflect and breathe.
2. Now imagine you are someone looking in from the outside. How are you feeling? What are you thinking?
3. Identify all of the big rocks, or priorities, in the situation you've chosen.
4. Organize the big rocks by priority. Not all of them will fit into the "jar" this week.

5. Break down each of the big rocks into more manageable pieces. Subdivide each large rock into smaller lists of to-dos using the Five Seconds at a Time technique. Do this in priority order.
6. Set a realistic timeline for accomplishing each goal. Place the most focus on what will get done by the end of the week and thus what needs to get done each day. Highlight items that need to be done today.
7. What will your milestones be? How will you reward yourself?

Possible Solution

List of Big Rocks (Priorities)

Personal: Improve physical health

Work: Create an effective workspace

Work: Understand responsibilities

Work: Determine what you need to learn

Work: Learn about Project Summit

Work: Establish a network and get to know people

Home: Organize house

Family: Spend time with spouse and children

Big Rocks Organized into Priority Sequence

Personal: Improve physical health. Because your back pain is slowing you down both at work and at home, taking care of it has to be your first priority.

Family: Spend time with spouse and children. You have always striven to put family first. Pat's soccer game is time sensitive and important to you, so it's near the top of the list.

Work: Create an effective workspace. Before you can accomplish anything at work, you need to be organized and have the necessary tools close by. Also, organizing should help you find the existing files on Project Summit.

Work: Learn about Project Summit. This seems to be important to your manager and has a deadline attached to it. Find out what you can about it as soon as possible.

Work: Understand responsibilities. Once these are clarified, you can break them down further and prioritize them based on profitability or on what your manager will value most. You do know that at least one of your responsibilities is Project Summit.

Work: Determine what you need to learn. This will help you act on your responsibilities. Once you know what you need to learn, you can make a plan for the months ahead for how to acquire the information.

Work: Establish a network and get to know people. Getting to know who your information resources are will be most helpful. Realistically, this cannot be accomplished in one week, so you'll want to keep it top of mind as a continuous goal.

Home: Organize house. As much as the disarray at home is burdening you, rectifying the situation will have to wait until the weekend or the following week since it doesn't have a deadline attached to it.

Big Rocks Subdivided into More Manageable Lists of To-Dos in Priority Order
(Many of these sub-points can be broken down into further sub-points.)

Personal: Improve physical health

- Look up massage therapy in the Yellow Pages or online.
- Choose a therapist and book appointment.
- Stop at pharmacy to get over-the-counter medication to treat pain in the meantime.

Family: Spend time with spouse and children

- Create reminder in your calendar to leave the office at five o'clock so you can get to the soccer game.
- Ask spouse to make dinner tomorrow so you can stay at the office a little later.

Work: Create an effective workspace

- Set up your voice mail.
- Obtain and organize necessary office supplies (pens, highlighters, paper, etc.).
- Skim through files to see if you can find anything on Project Summit.
- Post quick-reference tools such as phone lists and organizational charts.
- Sort through predecessor's files and organize in a way that you can quickly find what is relevant.

Work: Learn about Project Summit

- Set up meeting with Suzan to understand Project Summit and your role in it.
- Set aside "working" time to get the update completed by Friday.

Work: Understand responsibilities
- Create job description by drafting list of what you think your responsibilities are. Use employees or co-workers as resource.
- Review job description with Suzan, incorporate her feedback and have her sign off on it.

Work: Determine what you need to learn
- Learn system X.
- Learn program Y.
- Review policy/procedure B.
- Find out history of project C.

Work: Establish a network and get to know people
- Set up informal informational meetings with cross-functional managers in the month ahead to understand how your work affects the whole organization. Find out who your resources are. This will help you book follow-up meetings to obtain the information necessary to learn system X, history of project C, etc.
- Invite one colleague per week out for lunch to get to know each informally.

Home: Organize house
- Paint.
- Finish unpacking boxes.

Timeline for This Week

Personal: Improve physical health
- Today: Look up massage therapist in Yellow Pages or online.
- Today: Book appointment.
- Today: Stop at pharmacy to get medication.

Family: Spend time with spouse and children
- Today: Create reminder in calendar to leave office in time to get to the soccer game.
- Today: Ask spouse to make dinner tomorrow so you can stay at the office a little later.

Work: Create an effective workspace
- Today: Set up your voice mail.
- Today: Obtain and organize necessary office supplies (pens, highlighters, paper, etc.).
- Today: Skim through files to see if you can find anything on Project Summit.
- Tuesday: Post quick-reference tools such as phone lists and organizational charts.
- Next week: Sort through predecessor's files and organize in a way that you can quickly find what is relevant. (This is a time-consuming task, and the effort required may outweigh the results generated.)

Work: Learn about Project Summit
- Today: Set up meeting with Suzan for tomorrow to understand Project Summit and your role in it.
- Wednesday: Set aside "working" time to get the update completed by Friday.

Work: Understand responsibilities
- Thursday: Create job description by drafting list of what you think your responsibilities are. Use employees or co-workers as resource.
- Next week: Review job description with Suzan, incorporate her feedback and have her sign off on it.

Work: Determine what you need to learn
- Tuesday: Review policy/procedure B (you've learned this is linked to Project Summit).
- Next week: Learn system X.
- Next week: Learn program Y.
- Next week: Find out history of project C.

Work: Establish a network and get to know people
- Next week: Set up informal informational meetings with cross-functional managers in the month ahead to understand how your work affects the whole organization. Find out who your resources are.
- Next week: Invite one colleague out for lunch to get to know him or her informally.

Home: Organize house
- Next week: Paint.
- In two weeks: Finish unpacking boxes. Delegate part of this to your son, Patrick, and have an allowance tied to it.

VISION

1. Think about a time when you used envisioning techniques to successfully achieve a goal. Share your experience with your reading group.

2. Think about a performance you have to deliver in the near future (for example, a work presentation, musical performance or sporting event). Close your eyes. Take five minutes to envision yourself performing. (A work presentation is used for the example below.)

- Watch yourself standing up to deliver the presentation and quickly gaining the audience's attention.
- Listen to the exact words you are saying to the audience.
- Watch how your body language is engaging the audience.
- Watch the reaction from the audience once the presentation is completed.

3. Repeat the vision and correct yourself as you see things that should be changed. You may have to do this several times before you envision the whole performance with the results you desire.

4. Repeat this exercise several times before the actual presentation. After the presentation, reflect on how the technique helped you.

5. What are your own personal vision and mission statements? Your vision is your desired future state. Think possibility vs. probability. Your mission is the means by which you aim to achieve your vision.

Example of vision statement:
To make goodness fashionable.

Example of mission statement:
Endlessly strive for excellence by beginning each day with a plan and ending each day with a clear conscience, having lived with integrity, hope, proactivity, humility, courage, commitment and the full use of my talents contributing to others' discoveries and growth.

6. Take some time to think about a goal you would like to achieve (maybe a big rock). How will you achieve it? What steps are involved? What do success and the reward look like? Write your responses down. Then close your eyes and envi-

sion yourself successfully moving through each step and achieving it.

7. If the vision above requires the help of others, what are the key elements of followership that you personally need to improve on to bring your vision to life for others?

INTUITION

1. Think of a situation where you felt your intuition was telling you something important. Describe the situation.

2. In the situation above, did you act on your intuition? What happened?

3. Think of a time when you followed your intuition, but it led you to make a wrong decision. In hindsight, what factors led to your making the wrong decision? Did you collect an appropriate amount of information and exercise enough rational thought before making this decision?

4. When was the last time you had a great idea come to you out of the blue (for example, while you were in the shower, driving to work, etc.)? Did you act on this idea? Why or why not?

5. How can being more conscious of your intuition improve your creativity and decision-making skills?

6. How much time do you spend quietly reflecting and thinking without any distractions? What impact could setting aside a period of time for quiet reflection(for example, ten minutes a day) have on your life?

7. If you believe in a higher power, how does your intuition link to your faith? How could searching for God's plan strengthen your intuition?

POSITIVE THOUGHT CHOICE

1. Our daily thoughts are often negative. Write down negative thoughts you have had or negative statements you have made today or this week. Be honest!

2. How have these negative thoughts affected your well-being?

3. What attitude would be more helpful? What can you do to attain this attitude?

4. How will your thoughts correspond to your newly chosen attitude? Provide examples.

5. Henry David Thoreau described most people as leading "lives of quiet desperation." What do you think he meant by this? Does this statement have any truth in your life?

6. Write down a list of positive attributes you would like to be true. These should be specific—the more finished or complete the picture, the more specific the directions you are giving your subconscious mind. Write these truth statements in the present tense, as if the desired change has already taken place. When you tell yourself "I am going to," "I need to," "I want to," and so on, what you are actually telling yourself is "tomorrow," "later," "some other time." Examples of the present tense are "I am <u>organized</u>"; "I feel <u>in control</u>"; and "I can <u>succeed</u>."

7. Practise saying your truth statements out loud to your reading group.

8. Think of one of the most challenging situations you have ever lived through. Close your eyes and recall the emotions you experienced. How did you get through the situation? What did you learn through the experience?

9. If you were in the same situation again, how would your thought choices be different?

10. Think about a time when someone gave you a sincere compliment. How did it make you feel? How many times did you think about it that day? How did it affect your attitude?

11. How many times a day do you compliment other people or tell them how much you appreciate them? When was the last time you did this?

12. Former CEO of General Electric Jack Welch said, "Giving people self-confidence is by far the most important thing that I can do. Because then they will act." How can you positively influence the thoughts of others?

13. Write a list of things you are thankful for in each dimension of your life (for example, work, family, health, spirituality, finances).

FAITH AND ACTION

1. What is your faith or belief system? If you do not have one, is this an area of your life that may be beneficial to explore? Why or why not?

2. How can your faith help you accomplish challenging goals?

3. Was there a time when your faith helped you to accomplish your goals? If so, describe the situation and discuss it with your reading group.

4. The first component of faith is belief. How does what you believe about yourself affect the outcomes of your actions?

5. Why do you think trust is considered a step beyond belief? Do you put trust in the people in your life?

6. Do you have any fears that are keeping you stagnated? Fear is simply **f**alse **e**xpectations **a**ppearing **r**eal. How can trust help you let go of your fears?

7. What actions can you take to delegate better and trust others?

CORRECTION

1. Read the following statement by Dr. Maxwell Maltz out loud with your reading group:
   "Often the difference between a successful person and a failure is not one's better abilities or ideas but the courage one has to bet on his ideas, to take a calculated risk—and to act." Think of a time when you took a calculated risk and had a successful outcome. Why was taking this risk important? Discuss what you learned from the situation with your reading group.

2. Think of a difficult situation where you applied the "ready, fire, aim" approach. Was it successful? Discuss what you learned from the situation with your reading group.

3. Think of some difficult feedback you've received in your life. Discuss with your reading group your reactions to this feedback and what you did to implement correction.

4. Accountability is an important component of correction. When was the last time you openly took full ownership of a mistake? With your reading group, discuss this mistake and the impact admitting it had on the situation.

5. What necessary changes/corrections in your life are you scared of or will involve putting yourself in the discomfort zone? What techniques can you use to prepare yourself?

6. How will making this change/correction benefit you? What good will come out of the change?

7. What is your action plan to accomplish the change? First, brainstorm a few small, easy wins that you can accomplish today or this week. (Refer to Chapter 2 for help in breaking down your action plan into smaller steps.)

8. Who will support you through this change/correction? Consider asking your reading group to hold you accountable and to follow up with you at regular intervals.

AUTHENTICITY AND INTEGRITY

1. What does integrity mean to you?

2. What does authenticity mean to you?

3. Think of a specific situation in which your communication with someone was unsuccessful even though you said all the "right" things. On one piece of paper, write a sample of the exchange in the form of a dialogue. On another piece of paper, write what you were thinking but not saying at each stage of the interaction.[53]

4. The first dialogue may represent integrity. Does the second dialogue represent authenticity? Why or why not?

5. Read the following quotation:
   "Sow a thought and you reap an act. Sow an act and you reap a habit. Sow a habit and you reap a character. Sow a character and you reap a destiny."
   What impact do your thoughts have on your true character and authenticity?

6. Think of a situation in which you compromised your values to achieve a goal. Discuss what you learned from that situation with your reading group.

7. List ways that you can reduce the gap between your walk and your talk and better practise inside-out leadership.

8. Take some quiet time to reflect on the following. Do this somewhere close to nature (take a walk outside or look out the window). Turning on some soft music often helps inspire thought.

   - What is the purpose you have been called for?
   - What are your innermost values and beliefs?
   - Do you truly believe in the things you teach and promote, or are you just "talking"?
   - How can you be more authentic in the way you balance work and home and in the way you treat colleagues or family?
   - How can you better practise "servant leadership"?

HABIT

1. There is definite benefit in making time to identify the bad habits that are holding you back and not working for your leadership development. The following is a list of common bad habits that I have gathered from participants in workshops:

Place checkmarks beside the habits that you recognize in yourself.

❏ setting unrealistic goals
❏ answering email during family mealtime
❏ leaving for work without hugging the children
❏ ignoring problems
❏ losing things
❏ having your cellphone on day and night
❏ being a complainer
❏ using sarcasm
❏ avoiding delegating
❏ gossiping
❏ taking work home over the weekend
❏ giving advice that isn't asked for
❏ being late for meetings or events
❏ talking more than listening
❏ creating endless to-do lists instead of acting
❏ forgetting names
❏ not exercising regularly
❏ not cleaning your shoes

2. What did you learn about yourself from the exercise above?

3. How people see you on the outside often is much different from how you perceive yourself to be. It is humbling to remember that it is our outward behaviour that reflects the truth. Our inner perceptions are often illusions and rationaliza-

tions. Ask a family member, colleague, trusted friend or someone from your reading group to help you identify a habit you should change in your life.

4. What is one habit you have tried to change without success? Why have you been unsuccessful?

5. What impact would changing some of your habits have on your life? (Consider your personal, family, social and professional life.)

6. What is the benefit of not changing? (Note: There must be some benefit to not changing—or you would have changed already.)

7. If you don't change, what would be the impact on your future?

8. Which habit(s) will you commit to changing?

9. When and why did you first start engaging in this/these habit(s)? What do the answers teach you about your habit?

10. What is your competing response to the negative habit(s)?

11. What can you do to take temptations out of your environment?

12. What potential obstacles are in your way? How will you overcome these?

13. What is your action plan for accomplishing the change? First, brainstorm all of the things you could do; then choose a few small, easy wins that you can do today or this week. Next, choose your long-term action items. (Refer to Chapter 2 for help in breaking down your action plan into smaller steps.) What will you do to reward yourself?

14. Choose a date to commit to starting the change. When will the change be fully rooted as a new habit? What are the milestones along the way?

15. Who will hold you accountable?

16. Identify one big rock that you would like to focus on developing into a habit. Return to question 13 to identify your action plan for accomplishing the change.

17. When trying to form a new habit, you must repeat the action for it to stick. You can track your progress by logging your new daily habits on a monthly chart. After you perform each action, check it off on the chart.

ACKNOWLEDGEMENTS

We owe many thanks and both have an "attitude of gratitude."

Tara and I began working together on *Five Seconds at a Time*
in 2004, while I was teaching at the Richard Ivey School of
Business and Tara was a student there. Our respective colleagues at the university inspired us to implement the case-
study approach to learning, training and development, and
for that we are grateful.

We owe many thanks to Brad Wilson, senior editor at
HarperCollins, who championed our book and shared in our
vision. Brad, thank you for your thought-provoking questions, creative ideas and sharp insight.

Worthy of special note is the outstanding editing work performed by Cathy Witlox. Your dedication to correcting errors
made in the initial draft, your exemplary attention to the
smallest of details and your perceptive questions made you

an absolute joy to work with. Thank you especially for working late at night in order to meet publisher deadlines.

Most important, Tara and I both give ultimate thanks to our Creator for life-changing experiences, for words, for wisdom and for making the impossible possible. King David was correct: "He can move mountains and he is mighty to save."

From Denis

Tara, I deeply appreciate your commitment to excellence and your perseverance, especially when significant changes were requested. I am sure it was relatively easy for you to elaborate on the key principles I initially identified because your own lifestyle, character and faith are congruent with my lessons learned on Mount Ruapehu.

Most deserving of thanks and recognition is my precious sister, Kathleen. Your courage, compassion and selflessness have been an inspiration and the prime motivation for me to record my mountaintop experience that so vividly reveals Bruce's loving nature.

I give special thanks to my wife, Mary Lynn. I met her six days after Bruce's funeral. She not only "picked up the pieces" but has also been the support underpinning this book. In hindsight, I have come to believe that the main reason I was rescued from the mountain was so that my life would be blessed in marriage beyond anything previously imagined.

Other family members have encouraged and supported me in completing this work, especially my beloved mother-in-law, Sarah; my children, Daniel, Michael, Joshua, Jordan and Angela; and my in-laws, Bill and Gayle.

Thank you, too, to Denise McIntyre, president of the Learning Edge, who has enabled me to share my mountaintop experience with hundreds of people attending workshops she has arranged. Her trustworthiness and loving nature make her a precious friend as well as an admired colleague.

From Tara

Denis, I am blessed to have been given the opportunity to work with you. Your belief and trust in my abilities has truly unlocked my talents. I admire your being an authentic model of all of the principles presented within the text. Your enthusiasm for life is contagious!

I would like also to recognize my husband, Jeff. Thank you for being my best friend and for loving and supporting me through many hours of writing. To my family and friends, who have provided loving feedback and input for *Five Seconds at a Time*, thank you.

Finally, I must acknowledge the blessing in adversity. To make a long story short, serious injuries I suffered in a car accident while I was in university led to this opportunity to work with Denis and to co-author *Five Seconds at a Time*. I am truly grateful—it's amazing how we can grow when we look for God's opportunity in the face of life's challenges.

ENDNOTES

1   Paul Boers, "Take Your Time," *World Vision Canada Child View Magazine*, Spring 2009, 22.

2   Ralph Keyes, *Timelock: How Life Got So Hectic and What You Can Do about It* (New York: HarperCollins, 1991), 244.

3   Kerry Spackman, *The Winner's Bible: Rewire Your Brain for Permanent Change* (Austin: Greenleaf Book Group, 2009), 84.

4   MBA 2010 Student (Confidential), email message to author, June 16, 2009.

5   Author Unknown. Adapted from The Learning Foundation, http://www.learningfountain.com/bigrocks.htm.

6   John Huey and Geoffrey Colvin, "Staying Smart: The Jack and Herb Show," *Fortune Magazine*, Vol. 139, Jan 11, 1999, 163–166.

7   Converge Consulting Group Inc, "Master of Cycle Time: Little's Law," March 17, 2009, http://www.converge-group.net/archives/283.

8   Steve Lohr, "Slow Down, Brave Multitasker, and Don't Read This in Traffic," *The New York Times*, March 25, 2007,

http://www.nytimes.com/2007/03/25/business/25multi.html. (Microsoft study by Shamsi Iqbal and Eric Horvitz.)

9 Michael Watkins, *The First 90 Days* (Boston: Harvard Business School Press), Human Performance Curve, 210.

10 Jim Loehr and Tony Schwartz, *The Power of Full Engagement* (New York: Free Press Paperbacks, 2003), 12, 32.

11 Maple Leaf Foods, "Product Recall Information," 2008, http://www.mapleleaf.com/en/market/food-safety/maple-leaf-action-plan/product-recall-information.

12 Gary Gabet (human resources manager, Maple Leaf Foods) and Juan Alvarez (quality manager, Maple Leaf Foods), interview by Tara Bradacs, January 14, 2009.

13 Spackman, *The Winner's Bible*, 38.

14 Bernie Zilbergeld and Arnold Lazarus, "Lui Chi King was Imprisoned for Seven Years During the Cultural Revloution," *Indus Asia Online Journal*, June 2, 2008, http://iaoj.wordpress.com/2008/06/02/liu-chi-kung-was-imprisoned-for-seven-years-during-the-cultural-revolution.

15 Lydia Ievleva and Terry Orlick, "Mental Links to Enhanced Healing: An Exploratory Study," *The Sport Psychologist* 5, no. 1 (March 1991): 25–40.

16 Ibid.

17 PEANUTS: © United Feature Syndicate, Inc.

18 Daniel Goleman, *Emotional Intelligence* (New York: Bantam Books, 2005), 54.

19 Ibid., 43.

20 Malcolm Gladwell, *Blink: The Power of Thinking without Thinking* (New York: Little, Brown and Company, 2005), 267.

21 Ibid., 118.

22 Ibid., 119.

23 Ibid., 141.

24 Oren Harari, *Quotations from Chairman Powell: A Leadership Primer*, http://govleaders.org/powell.htm.

25 Blaine Lee, *The Power Principle: Influence with Honor* (New York: Fireside, 1997), 187.

26 John Lorinc, "The Long, Winding Road to 'Eureka!'" *The Globe and Mail*, October 17, 2009, Section F.

27 Ibid.

28 Loehr and Schwartz, *The Power of Full Engagement*, 96–97.

29 Peter Drucker, "Managing Oneself," *Harvard Business Review* (January 2005): 1–2.

30 David Baum, "Change from Delight," May 12, 2009, http://davidbaum.blogspot.com/2005/05/waiting-in-bosnia_12.html.

31 Pat Hicks, "The 7 Mental Laws of Success and the 7 Keys to Unlocking Them," http://www.docstoc.com/docs/260976/The-Seven-Laws-of-Success-and-the-7-Keys-to-Unlocking-Them.

32 Story read by Patrick Stewart, *Winds of Change*, video published by Criterion, Toronto.

33 Jill Bolte Taylor, *My Stroke of Insight* (New York: Penguin Group, 2006), 153–154.

34 Bruce H. Lipton, "The Nature of Dis-Ease," *Uncovering the Biology of Belief*, November 5, 2009, http://74.125.113.132/search?q=cache:vKHy6-fUibQJ:www.brucelipton.com/articles.

35 Albert Mehrabian, *Silent Messages: Implicit Communication of Emotions and Attitudes* (Belmont: Wadsworth, 1981).

36 D. Martyn Lloyd-Jones, *Spiritual Depression: Its Causes and Its Cure* (Grand Rapids: Eerdmans, 1965), 20.

37 John Geiger, *The Third Man Factor: Surviving the Impossible* (Toronto: Penguin Canada, 2009), 129–130.

38 Ievleva and Orlick, "Mental Links to Enhanced Healing: An Exploratory Study," 25–40.

39 J.Z. Borysenko, "Behavioral–Physiological Factors in the Development and Management of Cancer," *General Hospital Psychiatry* 4, no. 1 (April 1982): 69–74.

40 Carl Hughes, "Effective Leaders Delegate," *LP/Gas Cleveland* 65, no. 1 (January 2005): 10.

41 Tom Peters, *Thriving on Chaos: Handbook for a Management Revolution* (New York: Alfred A. Knopf, 1987), 57.

42 Max DePree, *Leading without Power: Finding Hope in Serving Community* (Holland: Shepherd Foundation, 1997), 25–26.

43   Michael McCain, *What's Happening at Maple Leaf,* April 4, 2009.

44   Janet Whitman, "'Mr. Fix-It' Needs Fix-Up over Big Merrill Bonus; Thain Faces Subpoena from New York State," *National Post,* January 28, 2009, © Canwest Interactive.

45   John M. Darley and C. Daniel Batson, "From Jerusalem To Jericho: A Study of Situational and Dispositional Variables in Helping Behavior," http://www.aug.edu/sociology/Jerusalem.htm.

46   CN Tower, "Facts at a Glance," http://www.cntower.ca/App_UserFiles/Documents/Press%20Kit/The%20Straight%20Goods-%20Facts%20at%20a%20Glance%20Sheet.pdf.

47   Peter Senge, *The Fifth Discipline: The Art and Practice of the Learning Organization* (Broadway Business, 2006), 18.

48   Gerald F. Cavanagh, *American Business Values* (New Jersey: Prentice-Hall, 1990), 55.

49   Max DePree, *Leadership Jazz* (New York: Doubleday, 1993), 1–2.

50   Henk Aarts, Theo Paulussen and Herman Schaalma, "Physical Exercise Habit: On the Conceptualization and Formation of Habitual Health Behaviours," *Health Education Research* 12, no. 3 (September 1997): 366, 370.

51   William O'Donohue, Steven Hayes and Jane Fisher (editors), *Cognitive Behavior Therapy: Applying Empirically Supported Techniques in Your Practice.* (New York: Wiley, 2003).

52   Rick Warren, *The Purpose Driven Life* (Grand Rapids: Zondervan, 2002), 308. Quoted by Dawson Trotman.

53   Adapted from Chris Argyris and Donald Schon, "Reciprocal Integrity: Creating Conditions that Encourage Personal and Organizational Integrity," in *Executive Integrity: The Search for High Human Values in Managerial Behavior,* ed. Suresh Srivastva (San Francisco: Jossey-Bass Inc., 1988), 197–222.